THE ANATOLIAN CIVILIZATIONS MUSEUM

DÖNMEZ offset ankara

Painting of Old Ankara. Oil on canvas. 200 x 117 cm. Painter Unknown 17th century Amsterdam Rijks Museum.

2- Aerial-photograph of the Museum of Anatolian Civilizations and Its historical surroundings.

3- General view of the Museum Buildings at the beginning of the 20th century and after restoration.

THE HISTORY OF THE MUSEUM BUILDINGS

The Anatolian Civilizations Museum is located in the district called At-pazarı ("the horse market") to the south of Ankara Castle. The Museum occupies two Ottoman buildings which have been renovated and altered to suit their new role. One of them is the Mahmut Pasha Bedesteni and the other is the Kurshunlu Han.

It is believed that the Bedesten (part of a bazaar where valuable goods were stored) was built between 1464 and 1471 by Mahmut Pasha, the grand vizier of Sultan Mehmet the Conqueror. There is no inscription on the building. Documentary sources, however, indicated that Ankara "sof" (cloth made from goat or camel hair) was distributed from here. The building has a plan of standard type. There is a covered rectangular area with 10 domes in the middle. There is a surrounding vaulted arcade, occupied by shops arranged so that those of the same trade face each other.

Recent research into the land registers and judicial records of the Ankara province show that Kurshunlu Han was built by Mehmet Pasha who suc-ceeded Mahmut Pasha to the post of grand vizier in the reign of Sultan Mehmet. He held the post until 1470, and he founded the Han to provide revenue for his soup-kitchen or the poor and needy in the Üsküdar district of İstanbul. He also built a mosque and medrese in Üsküdar, where finally he was buried. The building lacks an inscription, but during restoration work carried out in 1946 coins of Sultan Murat II were found, proving that the Han was in existence by the first half of the 15th century. The building has a typical plan for a Han of the Ottoman Period. In the middle there is a courtyard. It is surrounded by a series of rooms in two storeys. There are 28 rooms on the ground floor and 30 on the first. All of the rooms have fireplaces. In the basement of the west and south sides of the building there is a L-shaped stable. There are 11 shops on the north side, 9 on the east and 4 facing each other in the open-ended vaulted antechamber.

The two buildings, which are used as a Museum today, fell out of use after a fire in 1881

4- Inner and external view of Akkale
which housed the museum
between 1921 and 1949.

THE HISTORY OF THE MUSEUM

The first Museum in Ankara was established in 1921 by Mübarek Galip bey, Director of Cultural Affairs, in one of the towers of Ankara Castle called the "Akkale". In addition, objects were also collected together at the Temple of Augustus and at the Roman Baths. As a result of a suggestion by Atatürk that a Hittite Museum should be established, objects belonging to the Hittite period that were located in other museums began to be sent to Ankara. The need thus arose for a larger museum. Dr. Hamit Zübayr Koşay, Director of Cultural Affairs, submitted a proposal to Saffet Arıkan, the Minister of Education, stating that the Mehmet Pasha Bedesteni and the Kurshunlu Han could be used after some essential alterations as a Museum. This proposal was accepted and work started in 1938. Restoration was only completed in 1968. However, after the work on the domed central room of the Bedesten had been partly finished in 1940, a start was made on the arrangement of display objects under the direction of Prof. H.G. Guterbock. This display was opened to the public in 1943 while other parts of the museum were still under construction. The restoration project of this part was drawn up by the architect, Macit Kural, and the restoration itself was carried oft by the architect, Zühtü bey, after competitive bidding. In 1948 the museum moved into the four rooms at the Kurshunlu Han, the restoration of which was then finished, thereby leaving the building at Akkale as a depot. The restoration and display projects of the shops around the domed area were drawn and carried out by İhsan Kıygı, an architect at the Monuments Department. Five of the shops were left in their original condition, but the walls between other shops were removed and a large surrounding corridor was created as an exhibition area. The Museum building took its present form in 1968. Today the Kurshunlu Han is used as the administration section. Located there are study rooms, the library, a conference hall, a laboratory and workshops. The Mahmut Pasha Bedesteni is used as the public display area.

The Anatolian Civilizations Museum is among the leading museums of the world on account of its unique collections of material. The archaeology of Anatolia from the Palaeolithic Age to the present day is displayed by periods in chronological order in the pleasant ambience of Ottoman surroundings.

5- Aerial-photograph of Ankara Castle and Its surroundings.

6- A view of the ticket desk, bookshop, souvenir and rest areas.

7- A view of the inner hall of the Museum. The relief blocks "orthostad" and statues
are exhibited in their orginal architectural position.

8- General view of the Karain Cave.

THE PALAEOLITHIC AGE

The Palaeolithic Age or Old Stone Age began nearly 2 million years ago and lasted until 10.000 years ago. This is a general time-scale, valid for the world as a whole, but the exact length of the Palaeolithic Age varies from region to region. During this long period of prehistory early man first appeared. By producing the first tools he took the first, all-important step on the road of evolution.

Palaeolithic Man, whose existence was constantly threatened by natural and environmental pressures, lived in hunting and gathering groups. Mankind did not yet know how to grow crops but survived by gathering wild vegetables, fruits and roots and by eating the meat of the animals he hunted. As a result of climatic and environmental changes people migrated from one place to another, following the animals they hunted and searching for new supplies of food. They used caves and rock shelters as dwellings whenever they could find such places. Elsewhere they made shelters for themselves as best they could out in the open.

The Palaeolithic Age is divided into three phases, Lower, Middle and Upper, each distinguished by a number of characteristic features.

Drawing on his limited intelligence, Lower Palaeolithic Man started to fashion stone into simple tools and weapons in order to protect himself from wild animals, to feed himself, to hunt and at times to fight his fellows. The stone tools were usually shaped by using other harder stones, or were stones which required very little reworking.

The temperate climate of the Lower Palaeolithic Age was replaced in the Middle Palaeolithic Age by drier, harsher weather with heavy snowfalls, which led to a glacial period. This brought about a change in man's life-style and technological abilities. The most striking change in technology is shown in the stone tools. The rough, double-sided stone tools of the Lower Palaeolithic Age were replaced by tools which were properly worked. There were also innovations in the shapes of the tools.

By means of retouching on the edges, Palaeolithic Man obtained end, cutting, and scraping tools. In the Middle Palaeolithic Age Neanderthal Man was able to hunt the larger animals such as mammoths, rhinoceroses and deer. Although he used only hand-held weapons, it does prove that he had the necessary skills and tools for hunting.

During the Middle Palaeolithic Age we also find evidence for ritual practices. For example, graves comprising one or two pits were found to have places next to them where food was deposited. These show us something of the burial-customs of Neanderthal Man.

In the Upper Palaeolithic Age, when the weather again turned cold and dry, Homo Sapiens, the ancestor of modern man, replaced Neanderthal Man. Homo Sapiens was more akin to modern, intelligent man.

Stone-cutting reached the peak of its technical skill in the Upper Palaeolithic Age. The classic double-sided tools (handaxes) which were used throughout the Lower Palaeolithic Age and for part of the Middle Palaeolithic Age were replaced by various types of tools made from flint, blades and flakes. Scrapers, stone drills, chisels, leaf-shaped arrowheads and weaving-shuttles are some examples of these tools. In the latter stages of the Upper Palaeolithic Age flakes with overlapping backs were found.

As well as stone tools, a great many tools were made from bone and horn. Also at this time a number of stone tools were made solely for use in shaping bone tools. This shows us that in the upper Palaeolithic Age the production of tools for making other tools had already started.

Another important development in the Upper Palaeolithic Age was the creation of artistic objects which relate to man's intellectual life. Multi-coloured paintings, sketches and scenes in low reliefs made on cave walls and on various objects, including statues, demonstrate the role of Palaeolithic Art in the history of art generally. In the Upper Palaeolithic Age the production of ornaments also started. We know that fish bones, shells and the bones and teeth of various animals were being used for ornaments by that time. The burial of the dead was arranged in an orderly fashion in this period.

Although the Palaeolithic Age in Anatolia is not fully understood from the results of excavation and survey work so far undertaken, it is clear from the finds of stone and bone tools, from the human, plant and animal remains, and from the artistic objects belonging to all the stages of the Palaeolithic Age that Anatolia was very densely populated throughout the Palaeolithic Age.

Karain is the only cave at present known in Anatolia where all the phases of the Palaeolithic Age are represented without interruption. This cave, which is 30 km northwest of Antalya, contains a number of "habitation levels" of the Lower Middle and Upper Palaeolithic Age. In addition to the stone and bone tools, the small portable artifacts, teeth and bone fragments of Neanderthal Man and Homo Sapiens have been unearthed together with a large quantity of burnt and unburnt bone.

Karain cave is an important site for the Palaeolithic Age is not just in Anatolia but in the whole of the Near East.

The reason for our ignorance about many aspects of the Palaeolithic Age in Anatolia is that accurate methods of dating have yet to be perfected. Research, however, continues on the material found at the excavations and surveys carried out along the Lower Euphrates in recent years and on the re-started excavations at Karain and Yarımburgaz They are producing important groups of evidence that will help to solve the remaining problems of stratigraphy and chronology in the Palaeolithic Age.

The finest exhibits of the Palaeolithic Age in the Museum come from Karain. They include a variety of stone tools -hand- axes, scrapers and arrowheads. The bone tools include awls, needles and ornaments. These objects were found in deposit layers measuring 10.5 meters deep which represent all the phases of the Palaeolithic Age.

9- Karain Cave, Cavity E.
A view of the excavation
in 1986.

10- Karain Cave, Cavity E.
Earth formation 10.5 metres deep

11- Karain Cave, Cavity B.

12- Chipped Stone Tools.
Karain Cave Middle and Upper Paleolithic.

13- Çatalhöyük.

Mud-brick walls of Shrines.

Çatalhöyük, which 52 km.
south-east of Konya;
Is one of the most ancient
sites in Anatolia.
Excavated from
1961 - 1963, and 1965.

THE NEOLITHIC AGE

In man's prehistory the period in which the development of town-life started is known as the Neolithic Age. Neolithic Man knew how to produce food, but in the initial stages of this age the production of pottery was still unknown and so this period is called the "aceramic" period. At this time people used woven baskets, or wooden and stone containers. In Anatolia this phase has been identified at only a few sites. These first settled villages are represented by structures built in a fixed pattern, by stone or bone tools, and by weapons and certain ornaments.

The most highly developed Neolithic centre of the Near East and the Aegean World is Çatalhöyük, located 52 km southeast of Konya in the northern part of the Çumra Region. Excavations have revealed 10 different construction levels which, according to C14 dating, belonging to the period between 6800 and 5700 B.C. In these levels all the houses were built to a fixed pattern. This pattern was obtained by building rectangular houses next to each other around a courtyard. The houses were without stone foundations and had flat, mud-brick roofs. All of them were of the same plan: they had a large living-room, a storage room and a kitchen. The rooms were furnished with hearths, ovens and benches.

The main distinguishing features of the Çatalhöyük houses are the wall-paintings and bulls' head emblems on the walls. These decorations, most of which had cult associations, were not found in special buildings, but were located in a special area of the houses used for religious purposes. The bulls' heads were carved in high relief or made in the round, sometimes by covering an actual bull's head with clay. The wall paintings were on dull cream plaster and coloured in red, pink, brown, white and black. In addition to plain panels without any motifs, there were monochrome or polychrome geometric patterns, flowers, stars and solid circles. Scenes showing a number of different subjects were also produced. Among them were found representations of human hands, goddesses, human figures, hunting scenes and animal figures such as bulls, birds, vultures, leopards, deer, wild pigs, lions and bears. Other notable scenes include an erupting volcano behind a town, and a scene of human figures chasing away vultures that are pecking at headless skeletons.

These cult areas or shrines also depict a mother-goddess as a symbol of fertility. Figures of the mother-goddess were not only made of baked clay but also carved from stone. She is represented in various guises: as a young girl, an old woman or a woman giving birth to a child. Of these the figure of the mother-goddess giving birth to a child, supported on either side by two leopards, had a special significance. In addition to representations of the mother-goddess in figurines or in high reliefs, small terracotta models of animals were made as votive objects. The hand-made Neolithic pottery at Çatalhöyük was usually brown, black and red in colour. The pottery shapes are mostly oval and, in the late phase of the Neolithic Age, decorated with simple geometric motifs. Necklaces made of various stones and sea shells, obsidian mirrors and cosmetic articles show us how people adorned themselves at Çatalhöyük in the Neolithic Age. The earliest know surviving textile was found at Çatalhöyük. It can be seen from the wall-paintings that people used animal skins for clothing as well as textiles made of wool, animal hair or plant fibres. Stamp-seals, made of baked-clay or stone and decorated with geometric figures, provide the earliest envidence for claims of ownership in the Neolithic Age. Flint and obsidian were used to make various tools and weapons, while bone was used to make awls, needles and handles. Among the finds a flint dagger with a bone handle is particularly interesting. It was a grave gift. Although it was still not very common in this period, the working of copper and lead into artifacts was known. Trade also existed between settlements in Anatolia and the neighbouring regions.

The people of Çatalhöyük buried their dead under the floors of their houses. Children were buried under the floor of the room itself, while adults were buried, either individually or in groups, under the benches in the rooms. Grave gifts were placed beside the corpse.

Hacılar, which lies 25 km southeast of Burdur, is the second most important Neolithic site from which finds are displayed in the Museum. Only the four levels, IV to VI, belong to the Late Neolithic settlement (5700 - 5600 B.C.) out of the total of 9 levels that have been excavated. The houses at Hacılar, built on stone foundations with mud-brick walls, were like the Çatalhöyük houses but larger. They had red-painted plaster floors and walls. They had wooden posts supporting flat roofs and also stairs, showing that some of the structures were two-storied. In contrast to Çatalhöyük, the burials at Hacılar are extra-mural. Figurines of a seated or standing mother-goddess were found in nearly all of the houses.

The well-fired and glazed pottery of Hacılar is in red, brown and reddish yellow colours. The most interesting of the pottery exhibits are a red-coated glazed cup in the form of a female head and the rhytons in various animal shapes (deer, pigs, birds). Plant remains and sickles made of horn with flints embedded in one side reveal that the people of Hacılar knew about agriculture. Clay spindle whorls were also found, proving that textiles were being produced there.

14- Statuette of a Mother Goddess.
Baked clay. Height 20 cm.
Çatalhöyük.1 st half
of 6 th millennium BC.
The enthroned goddess is
supported by two felines and
is shown giving birth.

15- Statuette of Seated Goddess.
Baket clay. Height 4.1 cm.,
Çatalhöyük.1st half of
6th millennium BC.

16- Statuette of a Goddess. Black stone. Height 15.5 cm.
Çatalhöyük. 1st half of 6 th millennium BC.

17- Figürine of a Double Goddess. Marble.
Height 17.2 cm. Çatalhöyük. 1 st half of
6th millennium BC.

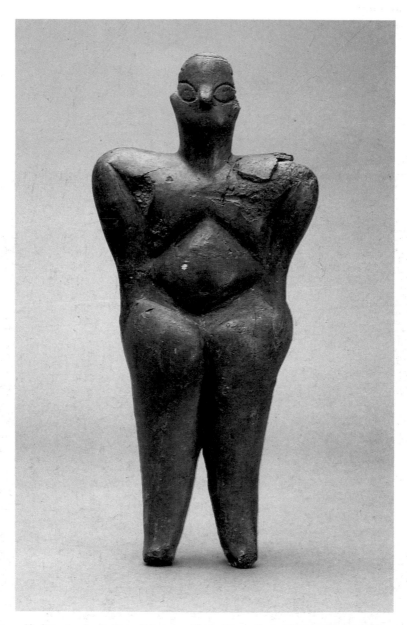

18- Statuette of a Goddess. Baked clay. Height 24 cm. Hacılar. Mid 6th millennium BC.

19- Strings of Beads. Stones-deer tooth and bone. Diameter, Different in size Çatalhöyük. 6th millennium BC.

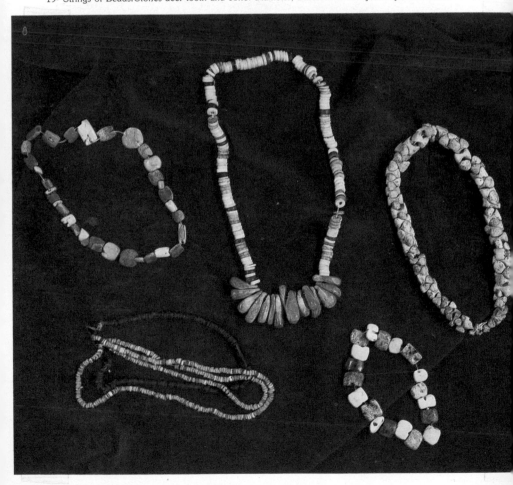

20- Mirror. Obsidian. Height 4 cm.
Çatalhöyük. 1st half of
6th millennium BC

21- Cosmetic Sets. Shell,
Bone and Clay.
Çatalhöyük. 1st half of
6 th millennium BC

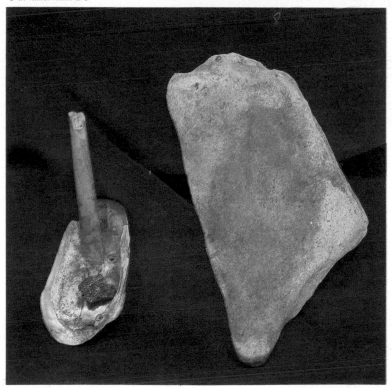

22- Deer and Man Figured Wall Painting.
Paint ornament on plaster.
Height 86 cm, Lenght 1.76 m.
Çatalhöyük 6th millennium BC.

23- Detail from the Hunting Scene
Paint ornament on plaster.
Çatalhöyük. 6th millennium BC.

24- Fragment from the Dancers Painting. Showing a hunter in white loin -cloth and black- spotted, pink leopard skin. Paint ornament on plaster. Çatalhöyük. 6th millennium BC.

25- A model room from Çatalhöyük.
The human relief-figure and bull's
heads have been reconstructed in
their original positions.
6th millennium BC.

26- Reconstruction of a funerary rite,
with priestesses disguised as vultures,
taking place in a shrine of level VII
at Çatalhöyük. 6th millennium BC.

27- A painted relief showing two leopards. Height 69 cm. Çatalhöyük 6th millennium BC

28- Wall-painting of a Great Red Bull. Paint Ornament on plaster. Height 1.19 m.; Length 3.35 m. Çatalhöyük. 6th millennium BC

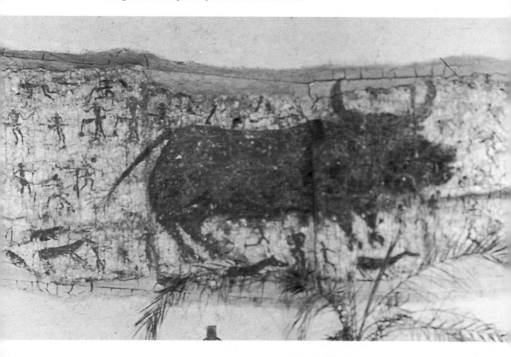

29- Small Cooking Pot
and Pot Stand.
Baked clay.
(Pot) Height 8,5 cm.;
(Stand) Height 7.9 - 8.6
Çatalhöyük
6th. millennium BC.

30- Four Footed Jar.
Baked clay.
Height 21.7 cm.
Çatalhöyük
1st half of
6th millennium
BC

30

31- Vessel in the Shape of
a Gazelle. Baked clay.
Height 13,6 cm.
Hacılar. mid 6th
millennium BC.

32- Cup in the From of
a Woman's Head.
Baked clay.
Height 11.1 cm.
Hacılar. mid 6th
millennium BC.

33- Stamp Seal Baked clay. Height 3.3 cm.
Çatalhöyük.1st half of 6th millennium BC.

34- Belt Clasp.Bone. Height (hook) 5.2 cm; Height (eye) 5.2 cm.
Çatalhöyük.1st half of 6th millennium BC.

35- Bone-Handled Dagger. Flin
Length 19.5 cm. (Handle) Bone. Length 10.3 cm
Çatalhöyük.1st half of 6th millennium BC

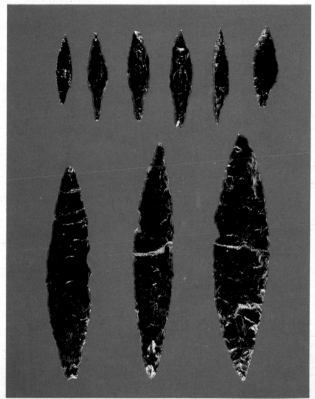

36- Lance Heads
and Arrow Heads
(Lance Heads)
Obsidian. Length
15.2 - 17.9 cm.
(Arrow Heads)
Obsidian.
Height 5 - 6.9 cm.
Çatalhöyük.
6th millennium BC.

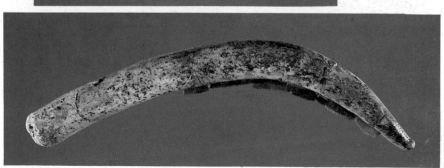

37- Sickle Antler. Length 27.8 cm. Hacılar, mid 6th millennium BC.

38- A view from Canhasan. One of the most important sites in Anatolia in the
Chalcolithic Age is Canhasan, 13 km. south - east of Karaman, near the Taurus
mountains. Canhasan was excavated from 1962 until 1970.

THE CHALCOLITHIC AGE

This period is called the Chalcolithic Age because copper started to be used as well as stone. It is clear from sites such as Hacılar, Canhasan and Kuruçay that there is direct continuity from the Late Neolithic Age. In this period, as in the Neolithic Period, distinct regional characteristics were still dominant. It can be divided into three sub-periods: the Early, Middle and Late Chalcolithic Age.

The most advanced example of Early Chalcolithic Age culture in Anatolia is seen at Hacılar. The houses, which were square or rectangular, had stone foundations and flat roofs. Hacılar had the appearance of a town, with narrow streets running between the buildings and with a circuit of mud-brick fortifications. The entrances to the buildings, placed next to each other in a row, led from spacious courtyards. These large houses contained a small cult room, a work area, a well and a pottery workshop.

The most distinguishing feature of Hacılar is its handmade painted pottery. In the Early Chalcolithic Age, levels V to I at Hacılar (5400 - 4750 BC), bright, glazed monochrome pottery was produced in advanced forms and with advanced techniques. There is also a great increase in the quantity of polychrome decorated wares that were being produced. The painted pottery is decorated with geometric motifs in reddish brown on a pinkish yellow ground. Oval cups, globular jars, large vases, rectangular bowls, jars and jugs are among the different forms that are known. The majority of the terracotta figurines of the mother-goddess, which are a continuation from the Neolithic Age, represent the goddess seated in a more stylized fashion. The stone and bone artifacts, together with a small number of copper objects, show the same continuity of traditions.

Canhasan, which is located 13 km to the northeast of Karaman in the province of Konya, is another site where the three phases of the Chalcolithic Age have been found (levels III-I). Canhasan lies on the natural route between the Konya plain and the Çukurova. The settlement acted as a commercial and cultural exchange centre between these two areas. The houses at Canhasan were rectangular, like the ones at Hacılar, and had walls decorated with geometric motifs. The cream or buff -coloured hand- made pottery was thin-walled. In addition to the monochrome wares, there are types painted in red or black and others decorated with lines filled with a white substance. Among the most important metal objects found at Canhasan are a copper bracelet, a copper sceptre -or mace- head and some copper fragments.

Another major Late Chalcolithic centre is Beycesultan in western Anatolia, 5 km southeast of Çivril in the province of Denizli. Of the forty construction levels excavated those between level XL and XX (4000 - 3000 BC) have been recognized as belonging to the Late Chalcolithic Age. Some of the rectangular, mud-brick buildings resemble houses of the "megaron" type. These contain pillars that supported the walls, fireplaces, bench- seats adjoining the walls and plastered storage rooms. One important group of objects found inside a clay vessel at Beycesultan comprises a silver ring, copper implements, a dagger fragment and three metal needles. Most of the Late Chalcolithic pottery is plain ware in grey, black or brown coloured clay, but some vessels are decorated with white geometric motifs or linear patterns.

The earliest sites in north central Anatolia belong to the Late Chalcolithic Age. Finds from the Chalcolithic settlements at Alishar and Alacahöyük are on display in the Museum. Excavations at Alishar, which lies 67 km southeast of Yozgat, have revealed levels XIX - XII as belonging to the end of the Late Chalcolithic Age. At Alacahöyük in the province of Çorum the corresponding levels are numbered XV - IV. At both sites the remains of rectangular mud-brick buildings and examples of brown, black and dark grey pottery were found. Some of the monochrome wares are decorated with grooved or incised designs. These wares are usually found in the shape of fruit bowls, jugs and jars.

The Middle Chalcolithic Age of eastern Anatolia is represented at the Museum by finds from Tilkitepe to the southeast of Lake Van. In addition to obsidian tools and supplies of the raw material, painted pottery called "Halaf" ware was found at this site.

During the Chalcolithic Age burial customs differed from region to region

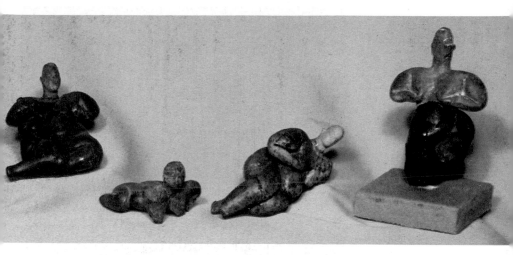

39- A Group of Statuettes of Mother Goddess. Hacılar, 6th millennium BC.

in Anatolia. Both the intra-mural and the extra-mural traditions are seen, but in both cases the bodies are buried in jars or in stone sarcophagi. The burials included pottery, ornaments and weapons as gifts to the dead.

Although Anatolia was densely populated during the Chalcolithic Age, a uniform culture had not been imposed over the whole area. Because of its geographical location, Anatolia felt certain external influences at this time. In northwest Anatolia the cultures of the Balkans and the Aegean islands made their presence felt, while that of northern Mesopotamia influenced eastern and south-eastern Anatolia and that of north Syria spread into the Çukurova.

40- Painted Vessel, Baked clay.
   Height 11.8 cm. Hacılar,
2 nd half of 6th millennium BC.

41- Painted Bowl, Baked clay.
   Height 8.8 cm. Hacılar.
   2nd half of 6th millennium BC.

42- Painted Pot, Baket clay.
   Height 11.2 cm. Hacılar,
2nd half of 6th millennium BC.

43 Painted Pot.
Baked clay.
Height 17 cm.
Hacılar,
2nd half of 6th
millennium BC.

44 Painted Vessel.
Baked clay.
Height 15,7 cm.
Hacılar,
2nd half of 6th
millennium BC.

45- Female Figürine, Baked clay. Height 32.5 cm.
Canhasan. 1st half of 5th millennium BC.

46- Painted Vessel, Baked clay. Height 26.5 cm.
Canhasan. 1st half of 5th millennium BC.

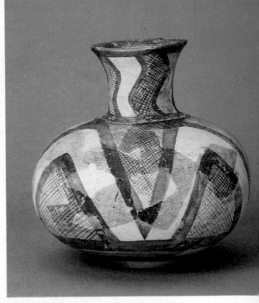

47- Painted Jar. Baked clay. Height 51 cm. Canhasan, 1st half of 5th millennium BC.

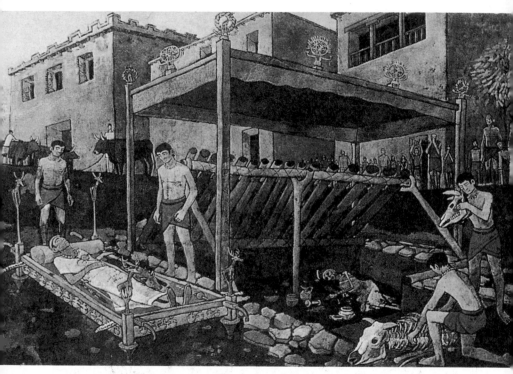

48- Reconstructions of a Royal tomb at Alaca Hüyük. The king lies upon a bier awaiting burial in a walled tomb in which the queen is already buried with her possessions and ornaments. 2nd half of 3rd millennium BC.

THE EARLY BRONZE AGE

The Early Bronze Age started in Anatolia in the late 4th millenium or early 3rd millenium B.C. At that time the people of Anatolia knew how to make bronze by mixing copper and tin. From this alloy they made all of their weapons, ornaments and utensils. In addition to bronze, they also used copper, gold, silver and electron (which is an alloy of gold and silver) to produce all the other objects they needed.

Many of the excavated sites, both large and small, show that people in the Bronze Age lived in settlements surrounded by defensive walls. These fortified cities appear to have contained buildings placed very close together. The houses, which reflect traditional Anatolian architecture, have stone foundations and mud-brick walls. They have square or irregular rooms furnished with hearths, furnaces and bench-seating.

Houses of the "megaron" type (long, one-roomed houses) can be seen at Beycesultan in the upper Meander valley. This type of building was in use for a long time in Anatolia.

The transition from the Late Chalcolithic to the Early Bronze Age was gradual and uninterrupted. The architecture of both town and village alike, the stampseals I and the idols continued to develop according to the local traditions. As in the Chalcolithic Age, the people engaged in crop cultivation and animal-husbandry made advances in the way they carried out these two all-important occupations. In addition, trade and metal-working also improved. Evidence for the growth in trade is seen in the distribution of goods over a large area. The working of different kinds of metal (gold, silver, copper, bronze, electron and even iron) was wellknown, and casting and hammering techniques had been developed. This is clear from the rich finds of metal, especially from graves, belonging to this period. Moulds used for casting have been found at sites, showing the advanced stage that had been reached in the technology of metal-working. The quantity and quality of the artifacts demonstrate that agriculture was not the only occupation at the time but that art and metallurgy were also important. The finds from Alacahöyük, Horoztepe, Eskiyapar, Kültepe, Mahmatlar, Kayapınar and even from Polatlı show very well that in this period metallurgy had gained as prominant a place as agriculture in man's activities. The manufacture and trade of metals had thus gained importance in this period. The largest centres of production were established in east and north-east Anatolia. If it had not been for this development in metalworking in Anatolia, it would have been very difficult to define the nature of trade in the Assyrian Colonies Period. The style of the metal statuettes, as well as reflecting man's beliefs and abstract concepts, is important since it demonstrates the development in metal-working and the artistic ability of the people of Anatolia. So, one can postulate the existence of a class of metal-working craftsmen in the Early Bronze Age.

An important centre that bears witness to the high leveh of civilization that was reached during the Early Bronze Age in Anatolia is Alacahöyük. The rich tombs discovered there are rectangular in shape, surrounded by stone walls and roofed with wooden beams. The skeletons are usually in the "hocker" position, with the knees drawn up to the stomach, and lie in the middle of the room together with the grave goods. Soil was placed on top of these wooden beams and plastered to make a flat roof, forming a house for the dead. The heads and legs of the oxen sacrified during the funeral ceremony were left on the roof. Sheep and goats were also among the animals that were sacrified. The sacrifical animals appear to have been associated with a feast for the dead. A dog was also left outside the tomb apparently as a guardian for the occupier. It is understood that the tombs, which continued in use for a long time, were intended for the royal princes who ruled the surrounding areas for several generations. The tombs belong to different occupation levels. Most of the grave goods are made from gold, silver, electron and bronze. There are also some objects made from amber, agate, rock crystal, iron and terracotta. The gifts found in the tombs include ornaments such as diadems, necklaces, needles, bracelets, buckles and earrings. Ceramic vessels were also found in the tombs. In addition, there are weapons made of bronze and gold, ritual solar discs, figurines of deer and bulls, goddess statuettes and sistra. The finds from Horoztepe, near Tokat, like the ones from Alacahöyük, demonstrate the wealth of the local rulers and the high level of metal - working that was reached in the northern regions. The finds from Eskiyapar, Kayapınar and Mahmatlar prove this from the point of view of the material, forms and symbolism of their artifacts. Parallels for some of the precious metal objects, idols and weapons are to be found made of fired clay, stone and base metal at almost every settlement.

From the excavations at Eskiyapar we can see that in central Anatolia precious objects were not only put in tombs as gifts for the dead but were also buried in the houses as treasure.

Bronze spear heads appear for the first time in Anatolia during the Early Bronze Age. Together with some types of axes, these spear heads and some of the other weapons have similarities to those in Mesopotamia and Syria. This can be seen from finds at Alacahöyük, Alişar Mahmatlar, Horoztepe and Dündartepe. The weapons excavated at Ikiztepe, near Samsun, provide a good example of the art of metal-working at this period.

The Alacahöyük and Horoztepe tombs belong to Kings of Hatti, the people who lived there at that time. The civilization and art are, therefore, known by that name. Finds from these sites include bronze figurines of bulls and deer; similar figurines decorated with a coating of electron; solar-discs on which the sun and rays are worked together; statuettes of bulls and deer surrounded by a solar disc; and other discs decorated with bulls' horns. There are also small female statues symbolizing fertility and motherhood, such as the statuettes from Horoztepe of a woman nursing her child, a small statuette from Hasanoğlan made of bronze, the head of which is gold and is plated with electron. All of these objects, like the sistra, are clearly associated with religious practices. Certain deities and divine symbols are first seen in the Early Bronze Age. For example, the motif of an eagle perched on a sistrum became very popular in the latter part of the period. These are the precursors of the solar discs, deer and bull cults and mother goddess statuettes found in the Assyrian Trade Colonies and Hittite Periods.

The handmade pottery of the Early Bronze Age is usually monochrome and only a very few examples have painted decoration. The decoration is usually in deep colours on a red or pale ground. The painted or incised decoration on the pottery always consists of geometric patterns. The principal types of pottery are beaked jugs, spouted teapots, large, black-glazed vessels decorated with grooves and geometric motifs in relief, one-handled bowls and cups, two- handled vases and jugs decorated with human faces. In the Late Bronze Age the forms of the fired-clay cups were very simple since they mostly take their shape from metal protontypes. At the end of the period there was a great increase in the number of the beaked pitchers, spouted and basket-handled teapots and angular cups and vases which imitated metal examples in clay. Most of these cup shapes are the first examples of the Hittite cup shapes seen in the later period.

In the Early Bronze Age the civilizations of western Anatolia, as in the other parts of Anatolia, had distinct cultural divisions and local characteristics. The topography of the region was one of the factors that gave rise to these differances. In the Museum the culture of west central Anatolia is represented by objects from Beycesultan and Yortan.

In the last phase of the Early Bronze Age trade links were established between central and western Anatolia. At this time the region of Troy was producing pottery in certain distinctive shapes, as well as ornaments made from precious metal. These items are to be found at important centres such as Beycesultan, Polatlı, Karaoğlan, Bozhöyük, Alişar, Kültepe, Gözlükule, Gedikli throughout central and south-east Anatolia. They are interesting because they indicate the area that was influeneced by the culture of Troy II. Together with vessels decorated with stylized human faces, the handmade, black cups of the Yortan type show that the common pottery forms of Western Anatolia had also reached the Ankara region. In addition to hand-made, monochrome vessels, wheel-made pottery also appeared in Central Anatolia in the last phase of the Early Bronze Age. There is also a new type of pottery which is known in archaeological circles "intermediate" or Alişar III" ware. This new type of pottery is hand-made and painted. Examples of this culture are most often seen in the southern parts of Central Anatolia.

Fiddle-shaped statuettes, made of terracotta, bronze, silver or stone represent a new type of the mother goddess figures produced in the Neolithic and Chalcolithic Ages. Another new group of objects which are seen in the southern parts of Central Anatolia in the last phase of the Early Bronze Age, are the alabaster figurines with round bodies, and 1 to 4 heads. They are usually associated with the painted pottery in sacred deposits or in graves and, up to now, they have only been found at Kültepe. These figurines are usually naked and are decorated with concentric circles and geometric motifs on their middles. Others are decorated with small-scale reliefs, most particularly lion and human motifs. These figurines, whose sizes range between 5 and 30 cms in diameter, represent the fertility goddess. There are also flat-bodied idols and figurines of naked women that are usually shown sitting on thrones with their hands on their breasts. They are always made of alabaster. They include examples that are worked out very naturally and show a stylistic development within a very short period of time. These finds from Kültepe have an important place in the evolution of the Anatolian style and shed light on a certain period in the history of local religions. They were produced in the last two centuries of the 3rd millennium B.C., together with the painted pottery of the Early Bronze Age.

The traditional Anatolian style stamp-seals that were used in the Neolithic Age continued through into the Early Bronze Age. They are made either of baked clay or of stone, but there are also a few made of metal. In this age the sizes of the stamp seals and of the motifs on them became smaller. The faces of the seals are convex and incised with geometric motifs. Loop-handles, with a vertical hole for a cord, continued in use. They also started to be put into graves as gifts in the Early Bronze Age.

The seals from Ahlatlıbel, Karaoğlan, Karayavşan are all very similar and a Mesopotamian influence can be seen on the seals found in southern Anatolia.

Among the Early Bronze Age finds there is a large quantity of spindle whorls, usually with some decoration, loom weights and wool spindles. They demonstrate that spinning and weaving were very much practiced in this period.

The cultures of eastern, central and western Anatolia had reached an advanced level of Civilization, each with its own local characteristics. External influences, internal relations between them and migrations did not effect these local characteristics. The most important feature of Anatolian civilization is that it preserved local characteristics throughout its history. In this period there were settlements throughout Anatolia, and the Anatolia peninsula was the culture and art centre of the ancient Near East. This period is represented by the rich finds in our Museum.

49- Stag Statuette, Bronze. Height 52.5 cm. Alacahöyük. 2nd half of 3rd millennium BC.

50- Bull Statuette, Bronze. Height 37 cm. Alacahöyük 2nd half of 3rd millennium BC

51- Ceremonial Standard.
Silver. Height 23.4 cm.
Alacahöyük. 2nd half of
3rd millennium BC.

52- Sistrum, Bronze.
Height 25.5 cm.
Horoztepe, end of
3rd millennium BC.

53- Ceremonial Standard, Bronze. Height 24 cm. Alacahöyük 2nd half of 3rd millenniuim BC These are the good examples of the cult objects, most of which are flanked buil's horn. All of them have been found in the tombs.

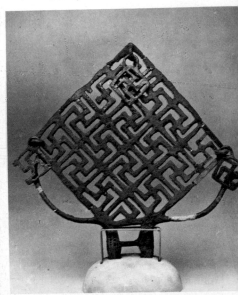

55- Ceremonial Standard, Bronze. Height 34 cm.
Alacahöyük. 2nd half of 3rd millennium BC.

54- Ceremonial Standard,
Bronze. Height 18 cm.
Alacahöyük. 2nd half
of 3rd millennium BC.

56-
Ceremonial
Standard
Bronze.
Height 23cm.
Alacahöyük.
2nd half of
3rd millennium
BC.

57- Statuette of Woman (Idol) Silver and Gold. Height 25cm. Hasanoğlan, end of 3rd millennium BC. Examples of the stylized female statuettes in the Early Bronze Age are made of stone. metal or baked clay. These statuettes symbolized fertility.

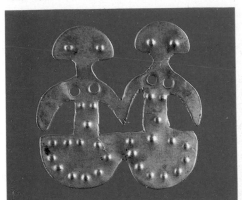

58- Twin Idol, Gold. Height 4 cm. Alacahöyük.
2nd half of 3rd millennium BC.

59- Statuette of Woman
Nursing a Child. Bronz
Height 21.5 cm.
Horoztepe, end of
3rd millennium BC.

60- Stylized Female Statuette, Silver.
Height 10.6 cm, Alacahöyük.
2nd half of 3rd millennium BC.

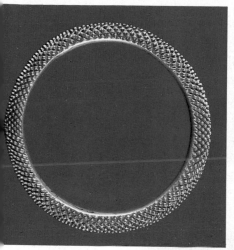

Bracelet, Gold.
Diameter 6.5 cm.
Alacahöyük.
2nd half of 3rd
millennium BC.

62- Mace Head, Gold.
Length 3.9,
Diameter 1.9 cm.
Alacahöyük
2nd half of 3rd
millennium BC.

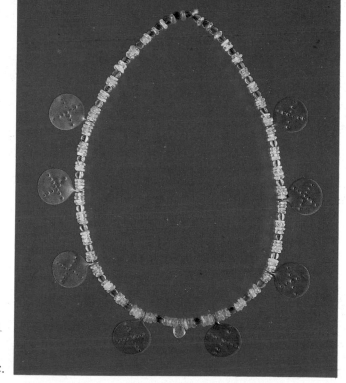

63- Necklace (Arranged)
Gold and rock crystal.
Diameter (disc) 3cm.
Alacahöyük. 2nd half
of 3rd millennium BC.

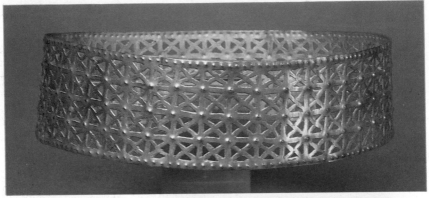

64- Diadem, Gold.
   Diameter 19.2 cm.
   Alacahöyük. 2nd half
   of 3rd millennium BC.

65- Hair Ornament, Gold.
   Length 2.4 cm.
   Alacahöyük.
   2nd half of 3rd
   millennium BC.

66- Belt Buckle, Gold.
   Length 15.2 cm.
   Alacahöyük.
   2nd half of 3rd
   millennium BC.

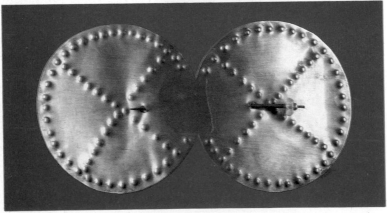

67- Pin with Head, Gold.
Length 18.5 cm. Alacahöyük,
2nd half of 3rd millennium BC

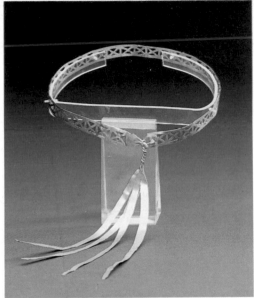

68- Diadem Gold.
Length 53 cm. Alacahöyük,
2nd half of 3rd millennium BC.

69- Belt (Arranged) Gold.
Alacahöyük. 2nd half
of 3rd millennium BC.

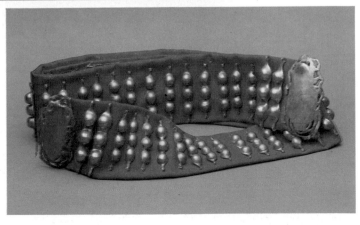

71- Handled Cup, Gold. Height 3.9 cm. Alacahöyük.
2nd half of 3rd millennium BC.

70- Necked Vessel, Gold.
Height 5.7 cm. Alacahöyük.
2nd haf of 3rd millennium BC.

72- Pitcher, Gold.
Height 14.3 cm.
Alacahöyük. 2nd half
of 3rd millennium BC.

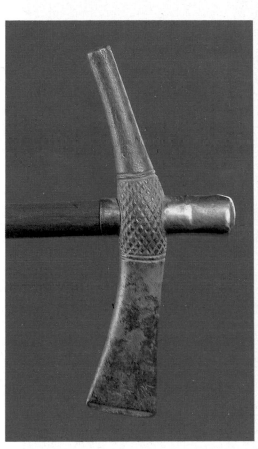

73- Composite Hammer and Axe.
    Bronze and Gold. Length 15.2 cm.
    Alacahöyük.2nd half of 3rd millennium BC.

74- Dagger, Bronze and Gold. Length 18.5 cm. Alacahöyük.
    2nd half of 3rd millennium BC.

75- Ceremonial Vessel in the Shape of a Human. Baked Clay. Height 28 cm Karataş-
Semahöyük. mid 3rd millennium BC. In western Anatolia, potters are continued the
traditional style of making different types of cups using the female form. This type
of cup is very widespread. Its origin lies in the Neolithic and Chalcolithic Ages.

76- Pot Baked Clay. Height 23.2 cm. Alacahöyük.
2nd half of 3rd millennium BC.

77- Beak-Spouted Pitcher Baked Clay.
Height 23.2 cm. Alacahöyük.
2nd half of 3rd millennium BC.

78- Quadruple Vessel Baked Clay. Height 7.5 cm.
Beycesultan Beginning of 3rd millennium BC.

79- Small Bell,Baked Clay.
Height 6.6 cm.Karaoğlan,
mid 3rd millennium BC.

80- Two.handled Goblet
(Depas Amphikypellon)
Baked Clay.
Height 22.2 cm.
Karaoğlan
mid 3rd millennium BC.

81- Wool Spindle,Bronze.
Length 20.4 cm.
Merzifon Region.

82- Stamp Seal, Baked Clay. Height 2.8 cm. Etiyokuşu.
2nd half of 3rd millennium BC.

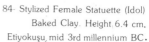
84- Stylized Female Statuette (Idol)
Baked Clay. Height.6.4 cm.
Etiyokuşu, mid 3rd millennium BC.

83- Stylized Female Statuette (Idol) Baked Clay.
Height 9.3 cm. Kalınkaya, end of 3rd
millennium BC.

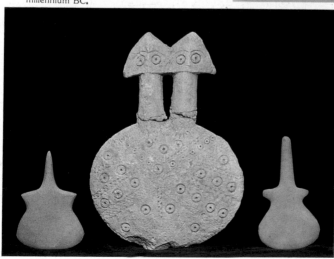

85- Idols, Marble.
Height 5.2 cm.
Beycesultan and
Kültepe, end of 3rd
beginning of 2nd
millennium BC.

63

86· Reconstruction of the entrance to the Assyrian Karum at Kültepe, a walled suburb almost one-third of a mile long. A caravan of donkeys are entering the Karum after checking in at the Anatolian city above and paying dues to the ruling prince. In the picture merchants are shown going about their business and scribes keeping their records on clay tablets which were subsequently baked.

THE ASSYRIAN COLONIES PERIOD (1950-1750 B.C.)

The beginning of this period marks also the beginning of written history and the Middle Bronze Age in Anatolia. In 1960 B.C. the Old Assyrian State which was located in northern Mesopotamia established a sophisticated trading system with Anatolia. In this period Anatolia was split up into a number of feudal city states, mostly governed by Hattians. Since the Akkadian Period the Mesopotamians had known about the rich resources of Anatolia. Now, under the initiative of the Assyrians, they established systematic trading relations with their neighbours in the north. The Assyrian merchants introduced into Anatolia their language, the cuneiform script and the use of cylinder seals. In 1950 B.C. thus began written history in Anatolia. The merchants employed donkey caravans for their journeys to and from Anatolia. They used the Diyarbakır, Urfa, Maraş, Malatya road or the Adana-Taurus route (through the Cilician Gates). They imported tin, goat hair felt, cloth, garments, ornaments and perfumes from Assyria and exported goods made of silver and gold. From the Anatolian rulers they acquired rights of security for their markets and goods and for the roads. They paid tax and rent on their activities. They had no political or military aims. They established their markets in Anatolia outside the cities where the local rulers lived. They had nearly 20 markets called "Karums". The central market was established at the Karum of Kaniş, in the lower city of Kültepe. All the Karums in Anatolia came under the control of the Karum of Kaniş. The Karum of Kaniş was responsible to Assyria.

The merchants from Assyria who came to Anatolia to trade lived together with the local people in the Karums. Most of the tablets that have been unearthed in the excavation of the houses where Assyrian merchants lived are preserved in our Museum. They are written in the cuneiform script. Apart from Kültepe, other centres have also produced such written documents. These records were kept on rectangular clay tablets written with a specially shaped stylus using the cuneiform script in the language of Old Assyria. The tablets and their envelopes were baked together after the envelopes had been written and sealed. The tablets mostly concern trading activities, but there are also some recording the private and social lives of the merchants.

During the Colony Period pottery was commonly produced on the potter's wheel, written history had begun and the Hittites appeared in Anatolia for the first time. The name of the king of Kaniş, Anitta, is known from a cuneiform inscription that was written on a bronze dagger. The dagger is among the finds from the Colony Period and is on display in our Museum. There are also various figurines of the fertility goddess, who was called Kubaba in the Hittite language, made from ivory, faience, lead and baked clay. The birth of Old Hittite art can be observed in these statuettes displayed in the Museum. The art of the Colony Period was generally a mixture of Hittite style with the traditions of Early Bronze Age and the influences of Hatti and Mesopotamia. This synthesis can be seen on the seals of the Colony Period unearthed at Kültepe, Acemhöyük, Alişar and Boğazköy. The cylinder seals and impressions produced in the Anatolian style and called the Anatolian group can be distinguished by their figural representations.

The art of this period is represented in the Museum by seals, small statuettes, mould-made lead figurines of gods and the gods' families and libation vessels (bibru). When the dress styles, weapons and helmets of the gods on the lead figurines are compared with Hittite deities, it is seen that the shapes of the helmets, horns, weapons, belts and short skirts are features known from the antelopes, pigs, eagles, cats, sharply pointed boots ad snails. In addition, we have in our Museum beak-spouted jugs, teapots and fruit bowls with multiple handles. The shapes of these cups were taken from the Early Bronze Age but with their very glossy, metallic appearance they are the most beautiful examples of this period. The painted pottery of the period is characterized by black, brown or red geometric patterns on cream surfaces.

Kültepe (Kaniş with its Karum), Acemhöyük, Alişar and Boğazköy are the principal Anatolian centres of the Colony Age. It is from these sites that the finds on display in our Museum come. There are very close similarities between these centres in the fields of city planning, architecture and small finds. The small finds, made of precious materials and found in graves or houses, represent the art of the period: gold objects and ornaments, bronze tools, figurines and vases made of ivory, obsidian and rock crystal. Ivory makes its first appearance in Anatolian archaelogy during this period. The ivory objects from the excavations at Acemhöyük and Kültepe are good examples ot their kind.

In addition, there are also displayed in the Museum seal impressions (bullae) and cuneiform documents that shed light on the history of the countries that were the neighbours of Anatolia in the Colony Period.

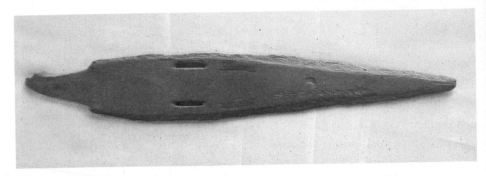

87- Dagger of King Anitta, Bronze. Length 29 cm. Kültepe. 18th century BC,

88- Spool, Bronze. Height 9.8 cm.
Kültepe. 18th century BC.

89- Spool, Bronze. Height 10.8 cm.
Kültepe. 18th century BC.

92- Statuette of a female deity, Ivory. Height 9 3 cm
Kültepe. 19th century BC.

90- Envelope, Baked clay. Height 11.1 cm.
Kültepe. 19th century BC.

91- Cylinder Seal, Lapislazuli. Diameter 1.3 cm
Kültepe. 18th century BC.

94- Figürine Mould, Steatite. Length 6.2 cm.
Kültepe. 18th century BC.

93- Figürine of a God, Lead. Height 6.5 cm.
Kültepe. 18th century BC.

95- Mould, Stone. Height 27.5 cm. Kültepe. 18th century BC.

96- Spouted Vessel and Three- Footed Pedestal. Baked clay. Height (vessel) 12.4 cm; (pedestal)
17 cm. Kültepe.19th century BC.

In this Age the potter's wheel was commonly used and new forms of pottery were introduced,
notably some new types of cup. Some of these cups can be seen in seal impressions.

97-Ceremonial Vessel with Relief of Human Face. Baked clay, Height 15.5 cm. Kültepe, 19th century BC.
There are numerous types of the monochrome and painted pedestal bowl. This ceremonial vessel
with relief decoration of a human face and horn-shaped handle shows the continuation in the 2nd
millennium BC. of the traditional style which can be seen in Early Bronze Age.

98- Ceremonial Vessel (Rhyton) Baked clay.
Height 15.6 cm. Kültepe 19th century BC.

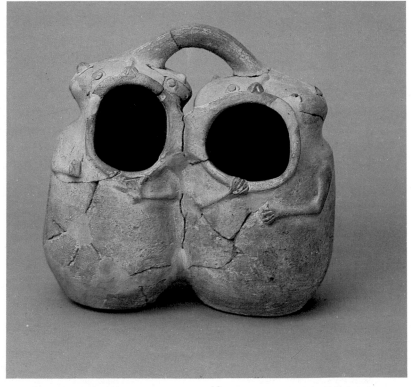

99- Double Vessel in the Shape of Two Human Figures Side by Side. Baked clay
Kültepe. 1st quarter of 2nd millennium BC.

100- Twin Ceremonial Vessel (Rhyton)
Baked clay. Height 5.5 cm. Kültepe
1st quarter of 2nd millennium BC.

101- Bowl with Animal-Shaped Spout
Baked clay. Height 46 cm.
Kültepe. 19th century BC.

102- Ceremonial Vessels in the Shape
of Lion (Rhyton) Baked clay.
Height 18.4-20.4 cm.
Kültepe. 19th century BC.

103- Beak-Spouted Pitchers, Baked clay. Height 47-24 cm. Kültepe, 18th century BC.
Good examples of beak - spouted pitchers can be seen in this Age. Most of them
were made on the potters wheel and richly painted.

104- Pedestaled Bowl. Baked clay. Height 42.5 cm. Kültepe. 19th century BC. Pedestaled bowls can be seen with one, two, four and six handles or without a handle.

105- Pedestaled Bowl.
Baked clay.
Height 21.7 cm
Kültepe.
19th century BC

106- Pot with
Animal-Shaped Spout.
Baked clay.
Height 23 cm.
Kültepe.
18th century BC.

107- Tub, Baked clay. Height 86 cm. Kültepe.18th century BC.In the tub there is a seat with two holes in it. It is hand-made.

108- Vase, Rock Crystal.
   Height 16.3 cm. Acemhöyük.19th century BC.

109-
Fragment of Vase, Obsidian.
Height 16.7 cm. Acemhöyük.
19th century BC.

110- Bullae. Baked clay.
   Diameter 1.8 cm.
   Acemhöyük,
   18th century BC.

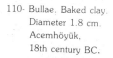

111- Box with Relief. Ivory. Height 10.3 cm.
   Acemhöyük.19th century BC.

112— King Tuthaliya IV the Embrace of the God Sarruma.This rock relief is on the one of the walls of the open air temple at Yazılıkaya near Bogazköy. These reliefs depicts a procession of all the gods of the Hittite Pantheon and display all the refinements of the Hittite Style. 2nd half of 2nd millennium BC.

OLD HITTITE AND HITTITE IMPERIAL PERIODS
(1750-1200 B.C.)

According to written records, Anitta, the son of Pithana, established the Hittite kingdom in the last phases of the Colony Age by uniting the Hittites then living in different city-states.

The capital of the state was moved from Neşa (Kaniş) to Hattuşa (Boğazköy) by Hattuşili I after the disappearance of the Assyrian trading colonies from Anatolia. This period is known as the Old Hittite period. The finds unearthed from the excavations at Alacahöyük, Eskiyapar, İnandık and Maşathöyük reveal that the art of the period remained faithful to the traditions of the Anatolian style. The pottery in the Hittite period, continued with only minor alterations the same shapes and techniques that had existed during the Assyrian colony period. The popular ritual - cups were produced in somewhat larger dimensions, as for example, the bulls' head rhyta found at Boğazköy and İnandık.

The tradition of making relief-decorated vases, which is known from the Colony Age continued; the best examples have been discovered at Eskiyapar, İnandık and Bitik. Before the excavation of these sites relief-decorated vases of this age had not been found. The İnandık Vase, which was decorated with relief motifs in friezes, is the finest example of this type. The common pottery shapes of the period were large bowls for washing, vessels in the shape of flasks, kantharoi, vessels with strainers and cult vessels in the form of goddesses.

One of two examples representing the state of metallurgy in this period comes from Boğazköy. It is a gold necklace in the shape of a seated goddess. The other is a bronze figurine of a deity from Dövlek. The bronze statuettes of Old Hittite figural art represent gods. It is known from written records that these figurines, which were thought to have protective powers, were kept in the temples.

The Old Hittite Kingdom's power was diminished for a time because of domestic power struggles, but during the second half of the 2nd millennium B.C., in the time of Suppiluliumas I, they regained their dominance and created an empire, that became one of the three most powerful states in the Near East, the others being Egypt and Babylon.

Examples of Hittite art, which reached a very advanced level in the Hittite Imperial Period, have been unearthed not only at sites in the Hittite homeland but also in all the Near Eastern cities which came under the domination of the Hittites or which felt the effects of Hittite political influence. The finds from the capital Hattuşa/Boğazköy, Alacahöyük, Eskiyapar and from all the other sites throughout Anatolia that were under the Hittite control constitute the most important collection of objects representing Hittite art. That these objects are fine examples of Hittite art is confirmed by the results of stratigraphic excavations, by stylistic similarities and by descriptions found in the written records of the Hittite period.

The emergence of Hittite Imperial art can be dated to about 1400 B.C. and continued without interruption until Hittite political power collapsed in 1200 B.C. During this period the finest examples of Hittite art were produced.

Hittite representational art describes the religious and historical events relating to the Kingdom between the time of Assyrian trading colonies and 1200 B.C. Events relating to everyday life also included religious functions since the sources of Hittite art were mainly religious and royal.

The plans and the construction techniques of the Hittite sanctuaries at Boğazköy display common characteristics. There are rooms and porticos around an enclosed courtyard. The statues of the gods were kept in sacred inner rooms called cellae. These Hittite sanctuaries formed the nucleus of grand establishments with a large number of staff. There are several gates in the city wall decorated with reliefs of deities, sphinxes and lions. For example, there is the relief of the War God at the King's Gate. The War God is worked in such high relief that it has the appearance of a statue. it is claimed in the Hittite records that statues of even larger proportions were also made in this period.

Another group of finds which are evidence of representational art in the Hittite Imperial Period are the stone orthostats (a row of upright blocks in the foot of a wall). The finest examples of stones used for architectural purposes are the Alacahöyük orthostats. Groups of decorated orthostats have not been found at any other centre apart from Alacahöyük. Religious subjects, such as can be seen on other examples of Hittite art, are depicted on these orthostats. The orthostats are on display in the central hall of the Museum.

In addition to over life-sized statues and orthostats, there are miniature figurines of deities made of gold, ivory, bronze and stone and small reliefs made in the same style. On these objects the gods are represented with large almond-shaped eyes, joined eyebrows, large (Roman) noses and smiling lips. On the reliefs the heads and feet are shown in profile whereas the bodies are shown frontally. These are all Hittite characteristics.

The tradition of the Old Hittite stamp seals continued into this period. In addition to stamp seals, ring seals and bullas came into use. There was, however, considerable development in the shapes of the seals and in the figural scenes. On these seals hieroglyphic writing was used together with cuneiform script, making them easy to read.

In the Imperial Period there is a decrease in the number of cup shapes and a regression in technology. Only vessels which have religious significance were carefully produced. The vessels in the shape of an animal, representing the two bulls of the Storm God, and the vessel representing the sacred precinct are particularly important.

One of the written records found at Boğazköy concerns the Treaty of Kadeş? (DATE). It was signed after the Battle of Kadeş between the Hittites and Egyptians. It is the first written treaty known in Anatolia. The original of the agreement was cut on a silver tablet but duplicates were made on baked clay. These clay tablets are, however, are amongst the most important archival material. Another important document is a bronze tablet found at Boğazköy in 1986. This tablet is written in cuneiform script. It measures 23.5 x 34.5 cm and deals with arrangements concerning the frontiers of the Hittitte Empire. This is the first bronze tablet to be found in Anatolia.

114- Ceremonial Vessels, Baked clay
Height 14.5 cm. Kültepe
19th century BC

113- Ceremonial Vessel, Baked clay.
Height 8.9 cm. Alişar.
17th - 16th centuries BC.

115- Ceremonial Vessel,
Baked clay.
Height 13.1 cm.
Beycesultan.
18th - 17th
centuries BC.

116- Two-Handled Pot with Spout, Baked clay.
Height 16cm. Acemhöyük. 19th century BC.

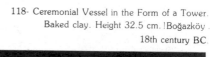

118- Ceremonial Vessel in the Form of a Tower.
Baked clay. Height 32.5 cm. Boğazköy.
18th century BC.

117- Quatrefoil Cantharos, Baked clay.
Height 19.3 cm. Alişar. 1st quarter of
2nd millenium BC.

119- Jug in the shape of Water-Bottle.
Baked clay. Height 49 cm. İnandık.
2nd millennium BC.

120- Ring-Vase, Baked clay. Height 30 cm.
Boğazköy. 14th century BC

121- Rim of Vessel in the Shape of a Tower,
Baked clay. Height (tower) 12 cm.
Boğazköy. 14th century BC.

122- Stamp Seal. Gold.
Diameter 1cm Kültepe.
18th century BC.

123- Beak Spouted Pitcher.
Baked clay. Height 45 cm.
Eskiyapar, 18th century BC.

124- Single-Handled Vessel
with a Sanctuary Model Inside.
Baked clay. Height 8.4 cm.
Eskiyapar. 17th-16th
centuries BC.

125- Vessel in the Shape
of a Bunch of Grapes,
Baked clay.
Height 14cm
Boğazköy.
18th century BC.

126- Ceremonial Vessel in the Shape of a Bull Head. Baked clay. Height 15.8 cm. Tokat, 17th-16th centuries BC.

127- Ceremonial Vessels in the Shape of a Bull. Baked clay. Height 90 cm. Boğazköy. 16th century BC. These vessels are in the shape of a bull symbolizing the Storm God, Teşup, of the Hittite pantheon. These are also cult objects which were used in ceremonies.

128- Figürine of
a Double-Headed Duck.
Baked clay.
Height 20.2 cm.
Boğazköy.14th
century BC.

129- Statuette of
a Seated Woman.
Bronze. Height 11 cm.
Alacahöyük.14th-13th
centuries BC.

130- Statuette of a Mountain God.
Ivory. Height 3.6 cm.
Boğazköy.
14th century BC.

131- Relief of
a God, Steatite.
Height 6.4 cm.
Yeniköy (Çorum).
14th-13th centuries BC.

132- Pendant in the Shape of
a Seated Goddess. Gold.
Height 2 cm. Boğazköy.
15th century BC.

133- Signet Ring,Gold.
Height 1.9 cm.
Alacahöyük.
14th - 13th
centuries BC.

134- Seal Impression of Urhi-Teşup,
King of Hittite,Baked clay.
Height 3.9 cm. Boğazköy.
13th century BC.

135- Cuneiform Tablet, Baked clay. Height 26.5 cm. Boğazköy. 16th - 15th centuries BC.The subject of this tablet is a ceremonial sacrifice. It is written in the Hittite Language in cuneiform script.

136- Statuette of a God. Bronze. Height 11.4 cm. Dövlek (Sivas). 16th-15th centuries BC. The statuettes and reliefs of Hittite art have a ritual purpose. This statuette of a young god is one of the best examples.

137- Relief of a
Warrior God.
Limestone.
Height 225 cm.
Boğazköy.

Relief of a god
in martial dress,
h a pointed helmet,
carrying an axe and
wore. It comes from
the inner side of
the King's Gate
of Hattusas.
14th-13th
centuries BC.

138- Orthostat Relief of Goats Being Carried to Sacrifice by a Priest. Andesite. Height 126 cm. Alacahöyük.14th century BC.

140- Orthostat Relief of Acrobats. Andesite. Height 116 cm. Alacahöyük.14th century BC.

96

-Orthostat Relief of a King and Queen Offering a Libation in front of a Bull.
Andesite. Height 126 cm. Alacahöyük.14th century BC.

Orthostat Relief of Priests. Andesite. Height 133 cm. Alacahöyük.14th century BC.
In Hittite art groups of orthostat reliefs are not found apart from at Alacahöyük. The
subjects of these are also ritüal.

97

Geç Hitit çağı beylerinden
WARPALAWA M.Ö. IX yüzy

142- Relief of King Warpalawas, Stone. Diameter 36 cm. Andaval (Niğde)

On the inscription accompanying the relief is written the name of one of the Late
Hittite cities Na-hi-ta. This may be modern city Niğde in Anatolia.

THE NEO-HITTITE STATES (1200-700 B.C.)

The Hittite Empire came to an end around 1200 B.C. as a result of the disruptions caused by the invasion of the so-called Sea Peoples. The Hittites who survived these invasions moved to the south and south east of the Taurus mountains and settled there. They were known as the Neo-Hittites. After this event they were unable to re-establish a centralized Hittite state, but Hittite traditions were continued by the rulers until 700 B.C., the year in which, after repeated attack by the Assyrians, they completely disappeared from history.

In excavations carried out at Carchemish, Zincirli, Malatya-Aslantepe, Sakçagözü, Karatepe and Tell Tayinat, important centres of the Neo-Hittite period have been discovered. Finds belonging to this culture have also been found at numerous other sites. These small city-states co-existed with the other political powers of the first quarter of the 1st millennium B.C.: the Phrygian Kingdom in northern and western Anatolia, the Urartian Kingdom in eastern Anatolia and the Assyrian Empire in northern Mesopotamia.

The Neo-Hittite cities were surrounded by defensive walls. The administrative and religious monumental buildings, placed on the highest point on each site, formed the citadel and the main protected area of the city. This was surrounded by additional defensive walls. The cities were planned as a single unit consisting of palaces, streets, monumental stairs and squares. The palaces were usually large complexes built around a courtyard. These structures, which were called "Hilani", were architectural features peculiar to the period. They were rectangular structures with columns at the entrances.

Another important characteristic of Neo-Hittite art was the incorporation of sculpture in architectural settings. The gates in the city walls and the facades of the palaces were covered with relief-decorated stone blocks (orthostats).

The region that they occupied lay on the trade routes to the Near East on the one side and to the Aegean Coast through the Central Anatolia on the other. Hence the influences of the Hittites and the Hurri-Mitannians, who arrived in this region in the second half of the 2nd millennium B.C., and of the Aramaians, who settled in the same region during the 1st millennium B.C., are clearly seen on the regional art forms.

In the Museum of Anatolian Civilizations, Neo-Hittite Art is represented by sculptures. The reliefs found on the city-gate of the Aslantepe near Malatya and the two lion statues form a group reflecting traditional Hittite features. On these reliefs there is a representation of Sulumeli, King of the Malatya region, presenting drinks to gods and goddesses. The statue of a Great King found at the entrance of the Aslantepe palace displays Assyrian features and is, therefore, dated to later period.

The most important city kingdom of the Neo-Hittites was Carchemisch in south-eastern Anatolia. Its importance was due to its location on the crossroads from Mesopotamia and Egypt to Central Anatolia. Most of the finds in the Museum are from Carchemish: the reliefs of Uzunduvar (long wall), Kral Burcu (King's tower), Kahramanlar Duvarı (wall of the Hero's) and Su Kapısı (Water Gate) are on display in the Museum in their original positions. On the reliefs various scenes are depicted: the religious ceremonies held for the Goddess Kubaba; the appointment of Kamanas, who was the eldest son of Arasas, the King of Carchemisch, as the heir apparent; the war chariots and victory scenes from the war with the Assyrians; and the gods and goddesses and various creatures of Hittite mythology. Both Hittite and Assyrian features are to be observed on the reliefs.

On the Sakçagözü reliefs, however, found at the entrance of the palace, Assyrian and Aramaian influences are very strong. They are, therefore, dated to the end of the 8th century B.C.

On the Malatya, Sakçagözü and Carchemish reliefs there are depictions of the Moon God. One of these shows the Moon God with wings on his head, and on another the winged Moon God is wearing a hat with a crescent on it. These reliefs indicate that the worship of the Sun and Moon Gods continued to be practised during this period.

Another common feature of the Neo-Hittite city-states was Hittite hieroglyphic writing. During this period the cuneiform script was no longer used. Its place had been taken by the Hittite hieroglyphs, which can be seen on such monuments as the Andaval relief and on the Sultanı-Kayseri and Köylüotu stelae, as well as on the Carchemish reliefs.

The Neo-Hittite Period is important in the archaeology and art of Anatolia as evidence for the survival of the Hittites until 700 B.C.

143- Pedestal of a Statue. Basalt.
Diameter 55 cm. Carchemish.
9th century BC.

144- Gate Lion. Limestone.
Height 124 cm.
Malatya-Aslantepe
10th-9th centuries BC.

145- Orthostat Relief. King Sulumeli Offering a Libation to God. Basalt. Height 86.2 cm. Malatya-Aslantepe 10th-9th centuries BC

146- Orthostat Relief of a Lion Hunt. Basalt. Height 53.4 cm. Malatya-Aslantepe 9th-8th centuries BC

7- Collosal Statue of King Tarhunza
Limestone. Height 318 cm
Malatya-Aslantepe 8th century BC

The arrangement of the wavy hair,
the treatment of the beard and
the tuft of hair on the nape
of the neck are Assyrian in style.
The king is bareheaded.
The finely made.
The sandals are faitfful
copies of Assyrian fashions.

148- Hieroglyphic Inscription. Basalt.
height 111 cm. Carchemisch 2nd
half of 8th century BC.

149- Orthostat Relief. King Araras with H
Son Kamanas. Basalt. Height 114.6 c
Carchemish 2nd half of 8th century F

152- Orthostat Relief. Soldiers. Basalt. Height 130 cm.
Carchemish. 2nd half of 8th century BC.

)- Orthostat Relief. The Children of King Araras. Bazalt. Height 119 cm. Carchemish 2nd half of 8th century BC.

151- Orthostat Relief The Wife of King Araras with Her Youngest Child and a Goat. Basalt. Height 115.2cm. Carchemish, 2nd half of 8th century BC.

153- Orthostat Relief. Officers. Basalt. Height 111 cm. Carchemish, 2nd half of 8th century BC.

154- Fragment of a Relief. The Goddess Kubaba.
Basalt. Height 82 cm. Carchemish 9th century BC.
An example of the traditional style.
The goddess is identified as Kubaba
by her horn and the pomegranate.

155- Orthostat Relief. Goddess Kubaba Enthroned on a Lion and Procession of
Women. Basalt. Height 90 112 cm. Carchemish 9th century BC.

156 Orthostat Relief. Procession of Men. Basalt. Height 100 cm.
Carchemish. 9th century BC.

157- Orthostat Relief. Battle Chariot. Basalt. Height 175 cm. Carchemish 9th century BC.
This Lock of hair occurs on every representation of a man's head in the Late Hittite style,
showing Assyrian influence.

158- Orthostat Relief. Sphinx with Human and a Lion's Head. Basalt. Height 133.6 cm. Carchemish 9th century BC. The best preserved reliefs in the traditional style come from Carchemisih. Their hooked noses indicate a Luvian or Hittite ethnic origin.

161- Pair of Sphinxes.Ba
Height 85 cm. Sakçagözü 8th century

162- Orthostat Relief, The Gods Sanctifing the Palm T
Under a Winged Disk.Basalt. Height 86.3
Sakçagözü 2nd half of 8th century

163- Winged Demon.Basalt. Height 86
Sakçagözü 2nd half of 8th century

164- Gate Lion.Basalt. Height 84
Sakçagözü 2nd half of 8th century

159- Hieroglyphic Inscription and King Katuvas Basalt.
Height 128 cm. Carchemish 9th century BC.

160- Hieroglyphic Inscription.Basalt.
Height 136 cm. Carchemish
9th century BC.

165- The whole area of Gordion, the capital of the Kingdom of Phrygia, is dotted with
tumuli of various sizes. The largest of these the Great Tumulus, is nearly 300 m. in
diameter and at present reaches a height of 50 m. The construction of the burial-
chamber and the grave-goods are much finer than those of the other tumuli.

PHRYGIANS (1200-700 B.C.)

At the beginning of the 12th century B.C., the Phrygians arrived in Anatolia from south-east Europe in the wake of the Aegean migrations. They laid waste all the important centres and brought-about the fall of the Hittite Empire. Then, gradually, they took over control of Anatolia. However, the main area that the Phrygians settled was the Sakarya valley which is bounded by the Afyon, Kütahya and Eskişehir regions. Gordion was their capital. The few surviving inscriptions of the Phrygians show that their language was Indo-European. The Greek sources, especially Herodotus, state that the Phrygians came from Macedonia where they were known as Greater and Lesser Byriges, while the Assyrian sources mention the Mita, King of the Mushki. It is now accepted that Mita and Midas are identical and the Mushki of the Assyrian sources are the Phrygians.

In the second half of the 8th century B.C. the Phrygian Kingdom became very powerful but, after the invasion of the Cimmerians at the beginning of the 7th centry B.C., their power declined. A short time after this event they came under the control of the Kingdom of Lydia. In 550 B.C. they fell to the Persians and lost their freedom completely.

The political life and art of the Phrygians developed in two stages: the Early (the period before the 7th century B.C.) and the Late (the period from the Cimmerian invasions in 695 B.C. until the last quarter of the 4th century B.C.). We know very little about Phrygian art in the early part of the first period, and most of our knowledge comes from the time after 750 B.C.

Gordion, the capital of Phrygia, was a fortified city surrounded by strong defensive walls. The public or official buildings of the city were constructed in the so-called megaron plan - rectangular buildings built in stone, mud-brick and wood- a technique which had been known in Anatolia since the 3rd millennium B.C. The Phrygians decorated the roofs of their buildings with geometric-patterned terracotta panels in the traditional style of Western Anatolia and covered the floors with polychrome mosaics. The finest examples of these painted terracotta panels in our Museum come from Gordion and Pazarlı. On these panels warriors, lion and bull fights, figures of creatures with human or bird heads and horse bodies, and goats on each side of the tree-of-life were depicted.

Apart from Gordion on the banks of the Sakarya river, sites in the bend and on the south of the Kızılırmak river such as Alacahöyük, Boğazköy, Pazarlı, Kültepe, Eskiyapar and Maşathöyük provide a good source of information for the Phrygians and their art. The rock monuments of Phrygia and the objects unearthed on other settlements show that Phrygian architecture had deep rooted traditions.

The families of the Phrygian Kings and the nobles were buried in built chambers made of juniper and cedar timbers and covered with a high mound of soil known as a tumulus. The wooden construction of these tomb-chambers show an advanced level of which wooden chambers were then built, and the space surrounding the chambers was filled with rubble. The roof was built after the dead body and the gifts had been placed in the wooden chamber. A large pile of stones was heaped over this roof and then covered with soil or clay to form the tumulus. Twenty-five of the nearly one hundred known Phrygian tumuli have been excavated. The richness and the variety of the grave gifts demonstrates the status of the buried person.

Apart from Gordion, important Phrygian tumuli have been discovered in south-west central Alnatolia, around Afyon and Eskişehir, and also near Ankara. Those in Ankara are situated in the Anıtkabir and Atatürk Farm districts. The tumuli belong to the periods between 8th and 7th centuries B.C. Their height differs between 3 metres and 40 metres. In the earlier periods dead bodies were buried directly in ground whereas in the later periods there was a tradition of cremation, the ashes being placed in special vases and then left under tumuli. The largest Phrygian tumulus is at Gordion. It reaches a height of 50 m and has a diameter of 300 m. The size of the wooden inner chamber is 6.20 m by 5.15 m. The room has a triangular pediment but has no door. The skeleton of a person 1.59 m in height and more than 60 years old was found on a large wooden couch in one corner of the chamber. This monumental tomb is thought to belong to King Midas. In it were found some large bronze cauldrons full of small vessels; they are set on bronze tripods next to wooden panels decorated in relief with geometric motifs. The small vessels in the cauldrons include omphalos bowls, bowls with swivel handles, buckets, small cauldrons and ladles, together with a large number of bronze fibulae. The Phrygians developed an individual style in making of cauldrons. They added their own concepts to those which were imported from the Urartians living in eastern Anatolia during the same period. The latter people attained a high level of metal-working technology, notably on the rims of cauldrons. The Phrygians used human heads fashioned in the Assyrian style whereas the Urartians used bulls' and lions' heads. The high level of workmanship seen in the geometric motifs that were made by engraving or inlaying techniques demonstrates that the Phrygians also attained a high level of technology in woodwork as well as metallurgy. The excavation of the tumuli has produced unique examples of Phrygians furniture decorated with geometric patterns, small figures of horses, small statues of bulls and lions fighting, and wooden relief panels showing mythological scenes. The Phrygians also produced ivory figures in their own distinctive style.

The individual style of the Phrygians is also to be seen in the "Cybele" figurines and reliefs and in the Cybele cult. Cybele, the chief goddess of the Phrygians, is to be identified with Kubaba of the Hittite pantheon in the 2nd millennium B.C. As a mother goddess she was the symbol of fertility and is usually represented with lions. The cult was introduced by the Phrygians to the Hellenistic and Roman world via Sardis. The "Cybele" figurines and reliefs in the Museum come from Boğazköy, Ankara and Gordion.

Another group of finds on display in the Museum are the andesite (a local Ankara stone) reliefs found in the Ankara region. On these reliefs the influence of Neo-Hittite and Assyrian styles can be detected. There are lions, horses, bulls, griffons and sphinxes on these orthostat blocks. These examples demonstrate the influence of Western Anatolian, Late Assyrian and Late Hittite styles on Phrygian art.

Phrygian wheel-made pottery is divided into two groups: the monochrome pottery and the decorated, polychrome pottery. The black or grey monochrome pottery produced in imitation of metal vessels is very common. On the decorated wares the patterns are usually reddish brown on a light-coloured surface. The motifs are usually rectangular, triangular, wavy or zig-zag lines, concentric circles and chequerboard patterns. Some of the wares were completely decorated with geometric patters. On some the patterns were divided into panels, decorated with animal motifs. Zoomorphic rhytons, reflecting the imagination and creativeness of the Phrygian artists, are a form of drinking vessel that had been in use in Anatolia since prehistoric times.

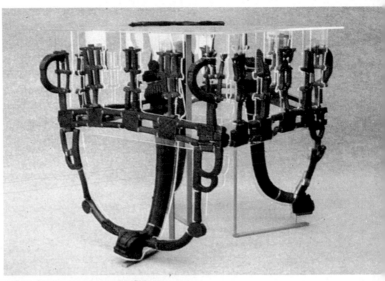

166- Table.Wooden. Height 64 c
Gordion.Great Tumul
end of 8th century B

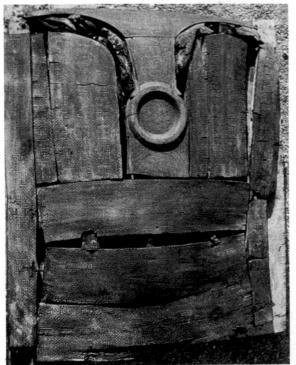

167- Inlaid table.Wooden. Height 94 cm
Gordion.Great Tumulus
end of 8th century BC

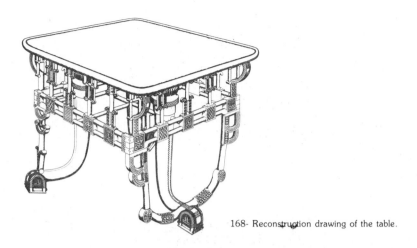

168- Reconstruction drawing of the table.

169- The construction of the burial-chamber beneath the Great Tumulus known as the tomb of Midas.

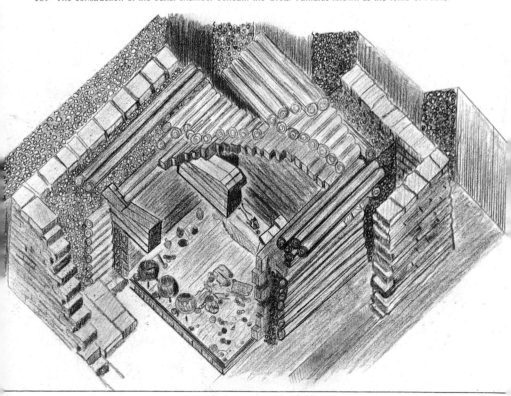

170- Round Mouthed Jug. Baked Clay. Height 30 cm. Gordion, Tumulus P end of 8 th - beginning of 7th century BC.

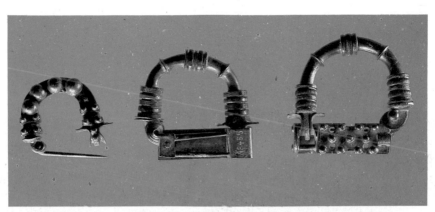

171 - Fibulae.Bronze. Height 5-6.5 cm.Gordion, Great Tumulus,end of 8th century BC

172- Sieve Spouted Jug.Baked Clay. Height 14 cm.Gordion, Great Tumulus,end of 8th century BC.

119

173- Ram's Head Situla, Bronze. Height 22 cm. Gordion, Great Tumulus, end of 8th century BC

174- Gander Shaped
Ceremonial Vessel (Rhyton)
Baked Clay. Height 37 cm.
Gordion, Tumulus P. end of
8th - beginning of
7th centuries BC.

175- Sieve Spouted jug
Baked Clay. Height 8cm.
Gordion, Tumulus W.
beginning of
8th century BC.

176- Small Cauldron and Ladle.Bronze. Height (Cauldron) 16 cm., (Ladle) 21 cm.
Gordion, Great Tumulus.end of 8th century BC

177- Pitchers with Single Handled.Bronze. Height 18-20 cm. Gordion, Great Tumulus
end of 8th century BC.

178- Goat Shaped
Ceremonial Jug (Rhyton)
Baked Clay. Height 16 cm.
Gordion, Tumulus P
end of 8th-beginning
of 7th centuries BC

179- Large Four Handled Jar. Baked Clay. Height 42 cm. Alişar 8th century BC.

180- Petaled Omphalos Bowl.Bronze. Height 5 cm.Gordion, Great Tumulus.end of 8th
century BC.

181- Miniature Quadriga Bronze. Length 16 cm Gordion, Tumulus P, end of 8th
beginning of 7th centuries BC.

182- Statue of Goddess Kybele
   Limestone. Height 126 cm.
   Mid 6th century BC

   The statue was found
   at Boğazköy.
   The mother goddess
   symbolizes fertility and
   prosperity. Her clothes.
   hairdress and her archaic
   features show
   Greek influence.
   She is decorated on
   both sides with figurines
   of musicians.

183- Relief of a Heraldic Design of Opposed Goats and Two Warriors. Baked Clay. Height 31-44 cm. Pazarlı. 6th century BC

184- Orthostat Reliefs, Horse and Lion. Andesite. Height 110 cm. Ankara, end of 8th century BC.

185- Fragment of the wall painting from the assembly-hall of Altıntepe near Erzincan. Two winged genii standing on both side of sacred tree. end of 8th beginning 7th centuries BC.

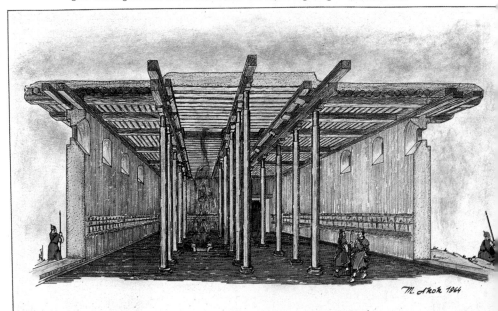

186- Reconstruction of the assembly-hall of Altıntepe, end of 8th- beginning 7th centuries BC.

URARTIANS

The Urartians established a state in the region of Lake Van in the early 1st millennium B.C. At its most powerful the sate of Urartu had a large territory in the land between lake Urmia and the Euphrates valley, extending from Gökçegöl in south Transcaucasia to the Araxes valley and from the east coast of the Black Sea to the borders of Assyria. The land of Urartu comprised plains and plateaus surrounded by high and rocky mountains with deep, narrow valleys. The Urartians, who had to adjust to harsh natural conditions, were successful in agriculture and animal husbandry. Eastern Anatolia, which supported agriculture and stock breeding as well as having rich sources of minerals, had attracted the attention of Mesopotamian peoples since very ancient times. Because of its wealth it was attacked many times by the Assyrians. The Urartians, who had to resist these attacks, became unified at the beginning of the 1st millennium B.C. and established the state of Urartu. The centre of this state was at modern Van (Tuşpa).

The name "Urartians" who disappeared after invasions from the north by Medes and Scythians in the 6th century B.C., first occurs in the 8th century B.C. in the records of Shalmaneser I, a king of Assyria. These were written in cuneiform script. The people of Urartu were neither Semitic nor Indo-European. Studies carried out on the Urartian language show that it was a dialect of the Hurrian language. A Hurrian civilization that was contemporary with the Hittites existed in east and southeast Anatolia, stretching westwards as far as Antalya. It covered some of the same territory as the Kingdom of Urartu 500 years before the foundation of the Urartian states. Thus it should be accepted that the Urartians were descendants of the Hurrian race. At first, Urartu was influenced by Assyria and used the Assyrian script and language. It became possible to read the Urartian cuneiform script because of two bilingual inscriptions on which the same texts were given in both Assyrian and Urartian. There are also a few official or commercial letters written in

Urartian on clay tablets. The written records of Urartu, however, were rather stilted, compared to those of Assyria. Urartian tablets written in cuneiform script mainly comprise legal contracts and letters. They are very few in number. The most important inscriptions are on stone, carved either on rock faces or on masonry blocks. They also had a script composed of figures like Hittite hieroglyphs. Urartion cuneiform records tell of the victories of Urartian kings, the slaves and spoils captured, and the building of canals, castles and sanctuaries. All these were specialties of the Urartians whose great accomplishments included the construction of water channels, making artificial lakes, irrigation works and the draining of swamps. This is confirmed in the Assyrian records. In their reports the kings of Assyria mentioned the fertility of Urartu and the wealth of the temples and royal treasuries.

The theocratic Urartian state was governed by a feudal system. In areas near the borders there were small city states governed by individual rulers, as in the earlier Hittite Empire. These rulers, who paid tax to the kingdom, were autonomous within their lands. They lived in fortified castles and in times of war their armies were put under the command of the Urartian kings.

Urartu reached the height of its power in the 9th or 8th centuries B.C. Although their kingdom was very mountainous, the Urartians tried to regulate the environment by public works, constructing dams and water channels. Besides these public works, the fine palaces and temples demonstrate the advanced level of architecture they possessed.

They cleverly adapted their monumental buildings to their surroundings. These were usually erected on very steep hillsides and carefully constructed of stones weighing 20 to 25 tons. Urartian architecture developed differently from that of Assyria. Urartian structures usually had stone foundations and long wooden beams. The temples, palaces, administrative building and castles with their workshops and storerooms were surrounded by city walls with many towers. These structures are examples of their monumental architecture which combines setting, plan and construction techniques. The structures unearthed by the excavation of Altıntepe, Çavuştepe, Adilcevaz and Kayalıdere and elsewhere are important examples of the construction works mentioned in the inscriptions of Urartian Kings. The temples and the palaces, with their multi-columned reception halls, mark the contribution of Urartu to the history of architecture. Altıntepe is the best example of this type. Another important feature of Urartian art is the wall-painting. Although the wall-paintings which adorne Urartian official buildings and monumental structures show strong influences from Assyrian art, they display differences in both pattern and style. The wall-paintings combine geometric and plant motifs with various animal scenes, all worked out in bright colours. From these wall-paintings, which date to the second half of the 8th century B.C. and the first half of the 7th century B.C., we gain an insight into the artistic interests of the Urartians. Although they lived in the harsh environment of eastern Anatolia, the most popular scenes on these wall paintings comprise plant and geometric motifs, sacred trees flanked by winged griffons, winged sphinxes, gods on sacred animals, animal contest scenes and various animal motifs. The use of bright colours make the paintings vivid. Red, blue, beige, black, white, and, very rarely, green were used in these paintings.

The helmets and shields that have survived bear the names of the kings who owned them. They are decorated with various figural and animal motifs. A bronze cauldron from Altıntepe had four bulls' head attachments. This cauldron belongs to the early 7th century B.C. Bronze cauldrons adorned with figures in typical Urartian style were exported to Phrygia, Greece and Italy. Decorated bronze panels. also had an important place in Urartian art. Belts, helmets, shields, votive plaques, harnesses and quivers can be included in this group. The most important characteristic features of the belts lie in the symmetry and repetition of the motives.

Seals constitute another important aspect of Urartian art. As well as stamp seals and cylinder seals, there are cylindrically shaped stamp seals. These show us that Urartian innovations were made with regard to seals. The seals portray animal, plant and composite animal motifs.

A tradition of ivory carving was also carefully preserved. Most of the ivory pieces found are fragments from furniture, and they demonstrate the importance of ivory. Among the finds of ivory are bird-headed winged griffons, human faces, stags in relief, plaques decorated with palmets, carved clasped hands and lion figurines. Among these the statuette of a crouching lion from a tripod stool in the largest lion figurine from the Near East.

Assyrian influences on the tomb chambers of the Urartian kings were considerable. The subterranean burial chambers of the Urartian rulers were hewn out of the rock. The bodies of the dead were placed in wooden or stone sarcophagi. Next to the burial chambers but very near the surface were simple rock-cut tombs and urn emplacements. It is thought that the kings' servants and slaves were buried in such places. There were, however, some urn emplacements in the burial chambers, which show us that both inhumation and cremation were practiced at the funerals of royalty and common people alike.

There is a rich collection of Urartian finds from Altıntepe, Ağrı-Patnos, Van-Toprakkale, Muş-Kayalıdere and Adilcevaz in our Museum.

187- Cauldron on Tripod Stand. Bronze. Height:(Cauldron) 51 cm, (tripod) 66 cm.
Altıntepe, end of 8th - beginning of 7th centuries BC.

188- Seated Lion Statuette, Ivory. Height 10 cm. Altıntepe. 2nd half of 8th century BC.

189- Winged Demon. Ivory. Height 12.4 cm. Altıntepe. 2nd half of 8th century BC.

190- Fibula.Bronze. Height 2.2 cm.Patnos 9th - 8th
centuries BC.

191- Votive Plaque.Bronze.
Height 15.7 cm.
Purchased,
7th century BC.

192- Quiver, Bronze.
Length 62 cm.
Kayalıdere, end of
8th - 7th
centuries BC.

193- Lion Statuette. Bronze.
Height 6.4 cm. Kayalıdere.
end of 8th - 7th
centuries BC.

194- Furniture Legs. Bronze.
Height 26 cm Kayalıdere.
end of 8th - 7th
centuries BC.

195- Stamp Seal.Gold. Height
1.2 cm.Patnos 8th century BC.

196- Cylinder-Stamp Seal.Steatite.
Height 3 cm.Patnos.8th century BC.

197- Seal in the Shape of Bell.Bronze.
Height 2.2 cm.Patnos.8th century BC.

198- Relief with a Sphinx.Gold.
Height 2.6 cm.Altıntepe,
8th century BC.

199- Buttons,Gold. Height 0.5 cm. Altıntepe, end of 8th - beginning of 7th centuries BC.

200- Vessel with Relief of Human Face.Baked Clay. Height 14.6 cm.Patnos,9th - 8th centuries BC.

201- Relief Base with Inscription, Adilcevaz-Kef Kalesi. Two winged gods standing on lions and facing each other. The figures are identified as Teişeba, the Storm God. 7th century BC.

202- Lion Statuette. Ivory. Length 29.5 cr
Altıntepe. 2nd half of 8th century B

203- Mask. Ivory. Height 2.6 cm. Altıntepe.
2nd half of 8th century BC.

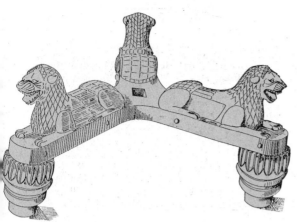

204- Lion Statuette in picture (202) is an ornament from a small bronze table on a tripod.

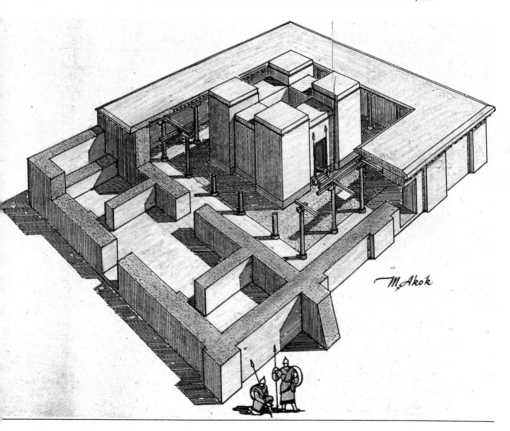

205- Reconstruction of the Urartian Temple at Altıntepe.

206- Sculpture Depicting a Boar Hunt. Marble. Height 83 cm. Ankara, 2nd century AD.

ANATOLIAN CIVILIZATIONS FROM THE 7th. CENTURY B.C. ON

"Dorian Migrations" at the end of the second millennium gave rise to the establishment of the first Greek colonies. The period between 1100 - 950 B.C. is called the "Protogeometric Age" and is characterized by ceramic objects shaped on wheels with motifs drawn by compasses. This 'Dark Age" of Central Anatolia lasted until 775 B.C.

The "Geometric Age" (950-600 B.C.) coincided with the alteration in western Anatolia of round shaped motifs into angular ones.

The term "Archaich." defines the period between 600-480 B.C. both in terms of time and of the architectural and sculptural characteristics of that period. The infrastructure of the "Classical" age of sculpture and architecture was set up in this period during which the "Orientalising" style, black and red figures were used.

The Carian, Lycian and Lydian civilizations which developed under the influence of the city states emerged in western Anatolia together with the Ionian civilization during the "Classical Age" which lasted until Alexander the Great entered Anatolia after crossing the straits of the Dardanelles. After Lydia was vanquished by the Persian Empire in 546 B.C., the civilizations in western Anatolia intermingled with Greek and Persian civilizations resulting in the creation of a Greco-Persian style in art. This situation ended with the invasion of Anatolia by Alexander the Great; and a new period started which is called the "Hellenistic. Age" (330-30 B.C.) lasting until 133 B.C. when the "Pergamon kingdom" came under Roman rule. Architectural and sculptural works, ceramic, metal and glass objects, jewelery and a great many coins belonging to those periods were added to museum collections either through excavations or purchase.

Objects made of marble, terracotta, gold or metal belonging to the period between the 1st century B.C. and the 4th. century A.D. during which Anatolia was under Roman rule have been found in the excavations undertaken by the museum (Roman Bath, Augustus Temple, Roman Theatre, Karalar, etc.)

Objects remaining from the Byzantine Age from mid fourth century A.D. up to the conquest of İstanbul in 1453 are numerous in the museum collections; however, the emphasis is on metal objects in display. The Seljuk and Ottoman periods starting from the 11th century A.D. in Anatolia are represented by coins

In this section of the museum, objects remaining from the Anatolian civilizations covering a period of about 2700 years from the 7th century B.C. on are being displayed in groups classified according to their material, the technical aspects of which are given below:

STONE OBJECTS:

Stone objects in the museum collections have either been found in foundation excavations and in archaeological excavations within Ankara or simply purchased.

Portraits or statues of gods, goddesses or administrators of Hellenistic and Roman Periods, hunting scenes, architectural elements covering the periods from Archaic to Byzantine, altars and tombstones are being exhibited either inside the museum or outside in the garden.

TERRACOTTA / MARBLE STATUETTES:

Hollow terracotta statuettes made by the moulding technique and small marble statuettes belonging to the Hellenistic and Roman Ages are found in Anatolia in large numbers.

The samples on display are the statuettes of Kybele the mother Goddess, which we already know from the statuettes of other Anatolian civilizations and from the monumental statues in Gordion and Boğazköy.

CERAMIC OBJECTS:

Ceramic objects shaped on a potter's wheel in the form of Greek vases and decorated with black and red figure technique on white background are more frequent in the Aegean region where the Greek colonies were settled, although they are very rare in central Anatolia in general.

Most of the objects exhibited in this section have been found in archaeological excavations carried out in Sinop.

METAL OBJECTS:

Statues and statuettes: Most of the small bronze objects are statues of Roman Emperors and various god and animal statuettes which were given as offerings.

The portrait of Emperor Trajan is among the important examples of "medal bust" (Tondo) style.

The first bronze statues were made by shoping the plate which was already riveted on to a wooden body.

Mechanical means such as riveting, hammering, twisting or nailing were used for shaping and attaching the plates to each other. Later, statues were started to be produced by casting bronze alloys into moulds. The fact that statues produced by this technique were heavy and expensive gave rise to a new technique which was convenient for the production of hollow, therefore lighter statuettes.

Ornaments: Ornaments, a subject of interest for women since the prehistorical ages, were originally made of stone, bone, sea shells and ivory. Together with the development of the metal work, bronze, gold, silver and electron were also used as the raw material for ornaments.

Bracelets, rings, brooches, necklaces, ear-rings, diadems and other ornaments on display belong to Greek, Roman and Byzantine Ages, have been added to the museum collections either through excavations or by purchasing. These ornaments, reflecting the fashion of the periods they belong to, were made by moulding, sealing, forging and casting techniques and decorated by filigree, granulation, enameling, repoussage, high relief and tula-work techniques.

Coins: The beginning of trade was in the of the exchange of goods. But later, as lumps of precious metals were started to be used in the exchange, the idea of money came up. These metal lumps in specific form and weight are called INGOTS in archaeological literature. The first coins were made by Lydians in western Anatolia during the second half of the 7th century B.C.

Due to the limitations of the exhibition area the rich coin collection of the Museum of Anatolian Civilizations cannot be displayed in its entirety. The ones on display are coins made in Ankara from the 1st century B.C. to the 4th century A.D. characterizing the history and monuments of the city and samples from Seljuk, Ottoman and the Republican periods.

GLASS OBJECTS:

As a result of archaeological researches, it has been found out that the first glass object were produced in Mesopotamia toward the middle of the 2nd millennium B.C., and the production was carried out in various centres using primitive techniques. Since the beginning of the 1st millennium A.D. remarkable changes were seen in both the production techniques and the forms. New forms were adopted to glass objects which were orginally peculiar to ceramics. Objects made by mould casting, massive cutting and mould pressing techniques were very few in number until late Hellenistic period, when the blowing pipe was invented and mass production started.

207- Portrait Head of a Tyrant.
Marble. Height 27 cm.
Karadeniz Ereğlisi. End of 6th
century BC.

208- Column Capital
with Lion (Funerary Stele)
Limestone. Ankara
2nd quarter of the 5th
century BC.

The name of Minos
is written on the stele
in Greek.

209- Portrait Head of a Woman.
Marble. Height 40 CM. Ankara,
Roman Theatre. 2nd century AD.

210- Portrait Head of a Woman. Limestone.
Height 33 cm. Mount Nemrut.
Late Hellenistic.

211- Statuette of a Seated Goddess (Kybele)
Marble. Height 25 cm. Purchased
End of 4th century BC.

213- Statue of Goddess Hygeia
Marble. Height 92 cm.
Eskişehir Roman
Period.

212- Statue of a Soldier, Marble.
Height 92 cm. Eskişehir Roman Period

214 Red Figüre Krater.
Baked clay. Height 26.5 cm.
Purchased, 5th-4th
centuries BC.

215- Red Figüre Pelike.Baked clay. Height 30 cm. Sinop
5th - 4th centuries BC.

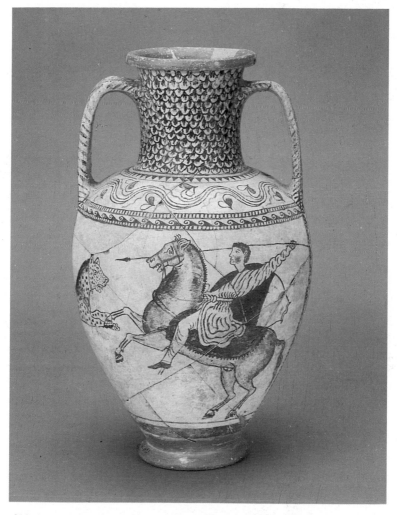

216- Amphora. Baked clay. Height 31 cm. Kültepe. Hellenistic Period.
   The body covered with a white slip with ornamental design painted in red and black.
   In the main panel a mounted hunter attacks with a spear a spotted panther. The hunters
   dress shows Eastern influence

217- Statuette of Herakles.
Bronze. Height 11.5 cm.
Yozgat Roman

218- Statuette of the Goddess Aphrodite.
Bronze. Height 12 cm.
Kırşehir. Roman Period.

219- Statuette of Zeus. Bronze.
Height 10.2 cm. Zonguldak Roman

220- Portrait Head of a Man. Bronze. Height 37 cm. Maraş.
1st half of 2nd century AD (Hadrianic)

221- Figürine of an Ox. Bronze.
Height 3.7 cm.
Havza (Samsun) Roman
Period.

222- Figürine of a Stag. Bronze.
Height 6.4 cm.
Safranbolu (Zonguldak) Roman
Period.

223- Figürine of a Bull. Bronze.
Height 9.5 cm.
Purchased. Roman
Period.

224- Portrait Bust of the Roman Emperor Trajan. Bronze. Diameter 63 cm. Ankara
2nd - 1st centuries AD.

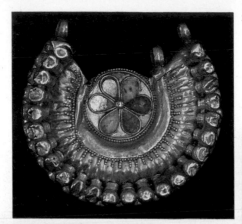

225- Ear-ring.
Gold and Enamel.
Diameter 2.5 cm.
Purchased. 4th - 3rd
centuries BC.

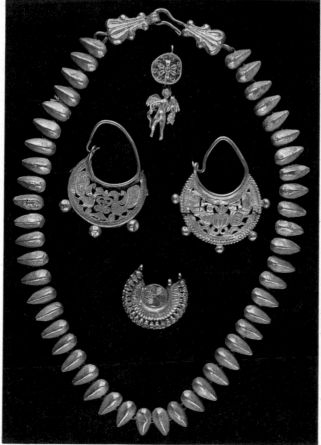

227- Pin with Head (Lion)
Gold. Length 6.5 cm.
Purchased. 4th century BC.

226- Neclace and Ear - rings.
Gold.Purchased.Byzantine
6th century BC.

228- Pair of Ear-rings. Gold and Plasm.
Height 3.5 cm. Tokat
1st century BC-2nd century AD.

229- Ear-ring with Sphinx Gold.
Height 2.1 cm. Isparta.
3th century BC.

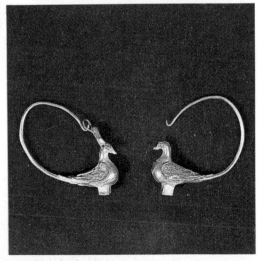

230- Pair of Ear-rings with Pigeon.
Gold. Height 3.2 cm.
4th. 3rd centuries BC.

231- Amphoriskos. Glass. Height 15 cm.
Taşköprü.End of 2nd century BC

232- Medallion (Phalera). Glass.
Diameter 3.8 cm. Purchased
1st century AD.

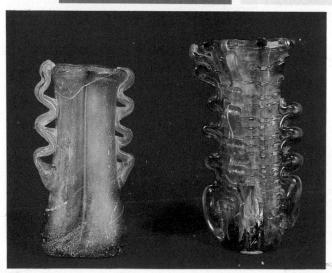

233- Double/Quadruple
Balsamarium. Glass.
Height 2-10 cm.
3rd - 4th centuries AD.

234- Perfume Bottles. Glass. Height 7.2 - 6 cm. Purchased. 2nd century AD.

235- Amphoriskos Glass
Height 13.4 cm. Hellenistic.

236-Statuette of Mother Goddess (Kybele) Baked clay. Height 14.5 cm.
Gordion Hellenistic Period.

ROMAN AGE CITY COINS OF ANKARA

1) AE-IMP. VESPASIANVS (A.D. 69-79)
1a) THE AUGUSTUS TEMPLE OF ANKARA

2) AE-IMP. NERVA (A.D. 96-98)
2a) THE AUGUSTUS TEMPLE OF ANKARA

3) AE-IMP. TRAJAN, KOINON OF GALATIA (A.D. 98-117)
3a) ANKARA AUGUSTUS TEMPLE AND THE STATUE OF MEN

4) AE-IMP. TRAJAN, KOINON OF GALATIA (A.D. 98-117)
4a) THE AUGUSTUS TEMPLE OF ANKARA

5) AE-IMP. TRAJAN, KOINON OF GALATIA (A.D. 98-117)
5a) THE TYCHE OF ANKARA CITY

6) AE-IMP. LVCIVS VERVS (A.D. 161-169)
6a) TOWER CROWNED BUST OF GOD SERAPIS

7) AE-IMP. SEPTIMIVS SEVERUS (A.D. 193-211)
7a) A STANDING WOMAN

8) AE-IMP. CARACALLA (A.D. 211-217)
8a) THE TYCHE OF ANKARA CITY

THE SAMPLE OF SELJUK, OTTOMAN AND TURKISH REPUBLIC COINS

AR. I. ALA ED-DİN KEYKUBAD (1219-1236. A.D.)

AR. II. GIYAS ED-DİN KEYHÜSREV (1236-1246. A.D.)

AV. SULTAN MAHMUD. I. (1730-1754. A.D.)

EV. FATİH SULTAN MEHMET. II (1451-1481. A.D.)

AV. ATATÜRK'S CENTENNIAL COMMORATIVE COIN.

BIBLIOGRAPHY

PREHISTORIC PERIODS
Paleolithic

BORDES. F. · Le Paléolithique Dans le Monde.
(1968) L'Univers des Connaissances, Paris, 1968
CHILDE. G. ·Man Makes Himself.
(1956) Watts, London, 1956
CHILDE, G. · ·Tarihte Neler oldu.
(1974) (Çev. Alãeddin Şenel - Meten Tunçay) Odak Yayınları: 10.
Tarih dizisi (T): 2 Ankara, 1974.
KANSU, Şevket Aziz: "Stone Age Cultures in Turkey",
American, Journal of Archaeology. vol. 51, 1947
KÖKTEN, I. Kılıç: "Antalya Karain Mağarasında Yapılan Tarih Ön-
cesi Araştırmalarına Toplu Bir Bakış", Türk Arkeoloji Dergisi VII-I
KÖKTEN, I. K.· "Karain'in Türkiye Prehistoryasındaki Yeri".
T.C.D XVIII - XIX, Sayı 22-23, Ankara, 1964, s. 17-27
SEMENOV, S.A.- Prehistoric Technology.
(1964) (Translated by M.W Thompson) Cory, Adams - Mackay, Lon-
don, 1964.
SOLECKI, R.S. "The old world paleolithic"
The Old World Early Man to the Development of Agriculture New
York, 1974 pp. 45-70.
SOYLU, G.· Prehistorik Devirlerde Avcılık ve Türkiye'deki İzleri.
(1971) Yayınlanmamış Doktora tezi. Ankara, 1971
YALÇINKAYA, I.· Taş Devirlerinde Sanat Eserleri ve Türkiye'deki
İzleri (1973) Yayınlanmamış Doktora tezi. Ankara, 1971

Neolithic Chalcolithic Early Bronze Age

ARIK, R.O.: Türk Tarih Kurumu Tarafından Yapılan Alacahöyük
Hafriyatı 1935, Ankara. 1936
ARIK, R.O. "Karaoğlan Hafriyatı" Belleten III., 1939
Avrupa Konseyi 18. Avrupa Sanat Sergisi, Anadolu Medeniyetleri, İstan-
bul. 1983. Tarih Öncesi / Hitit / İlk Demir Çağı, T.C. Kültür ve Tu-
rizm Bakanlığı.
BLEGEN, C.W. "Troy I. General Introduction. The First and Second
Settlements" Princeton, 1950.
Troy II. The Third Fourth and Fifth Settlements, Princeton 1951
DOLUNAY, Necati: "Hasanoğlan İdolü" V. Türk Tarih Kongresi Ra-
poru. TTK. Basımevi, Ankara 1960
FRENCH, D.H.: "Late Chalcolithic Pottery in North-West Turkey
and The Aegean", Anatolian Studies, XI, 1961.
FRENCH, D.H.: "Excavations at Can Hasan." Anatolian Studies, XII,
1962; "Excavations at Can Hasan : Second Preliminary Re-
port, 1962", Anatolian Studies, XIII, 1963; "Third Preliminary
Report", Anatolian Studies, XIV. 1964; "Fourth Preliminary Re-
port, 1964", Anatolian Studies XV, 1965; "Fifth Preliminary Re-
port", Anatolian Studies XVI, 1966
GÜTERBOCK, H.G.: Halil Ethem Hatıra Kitabı, Ankara 1947
KANSU, Şevket Aziz: Etiyokuşu Hafriyatı Raporu 1937, TTK, Ba-
sımevi, Ankara 1940.
KOŞAY, H. Z.: Alacahöyük Kazısı 1936, Ankara, 1944·
KOŞAY, H.Z: Türk Tarih Kurumu Tarafından Yapılan Alacahöyük
Kaısı 1937-1939'daki Çalışmalara ve Keşiflere Ait İlk Rapor, TTKY
S.V, no. 5, Ankara 1951
KOŞAY H. Z.: Akok, M., Türk Tarih Kurumu Tarafından Yapılan
Alacahöyük Kazısı 1940-1948'deki Çalışmalara ve Keşiflere Ait İlk
Rapor, TTK Ys. V., no. 6, Ankara-1966
KOŞAY, H.Z.: "Ahlatlıbel Hafriyatı" Türk Tarih Arkeologya ve Etnoğ-
rafya Dergisi, II, Ankara, 1934.
KOŞAY, H.Z ve TURFAN, K.: "Erzurum-Karaz Kazısı Raporu",
Belleten, XXIII, 1959.
KOŞAY, H.Z. ve VARY, H: Pulur Kazısı Raporu, Ankara, 1964
KOŞAY, H.Z. ve AKOK M.· "Amasya Mahmatlar Köyü Definesi"
Belleten. XIV. 1950
LLOYD, S. ve MELLAART, J.: Beycesultan I, The Chalcolithic and
Early Bronze Age Levels, London, 1962
MELLAART, James: "Anatolian Chronology in the Early and Middle
Bronze Age", Anatolian Studies, VII, 1957.

MELLAART, James: "Early Cultures of the South Anatolian Plateau.
The Late Chalcolithic and Early Bronze Ages in the Konya Pla-
in", Anatolian Studies, XIII, 1963
MELLAART, James: Çatalhöyük. A Neolithic Town in Anatolia,
London, 1967.
MELLAART, James: Excavations at Hacılar, vol. I-II
MELLINK, M.J.: "Excavations at Karataş-Semayük in Lycia, 1963"
American Journal of Archoeology, 68, 1964;
"Excavations at Karataş-Semayük, 1964" AJA, 69, 1965
"Excavations at Karataş-Semayük, 1965", AJA, 70, 1966
"Excavations at Karataş-Semayük, 1966", AJA, 71, 1967
MELLINK, M. J.: "The Royal Tombs at Alacahöyük. The Aegean
and The Near East", Studies Present to Hetty Goldman, New York,
1956.
ORTHMANN, Winifred: Die Keramik der Frühen Bronzezelt aus
Inneranatolian, Berlin, 1963
ÖZGÜÇ, Tahsin ve AKOK, M.: Horoztepe, TTK. Basımevi-Ankara,
1958.
ÖZGÜÇ, Tahsin: "Yeni Araştırmaların Işığında Eski Anadolu Arkeo-
lojisi". Anatolia VII, 1963 (1964), 23-42.
ÖZGÜÇ, Tahsin: "Çorum Çevresinde Bulunan Eski Tunç Çağı Eser-
leri" TTK Belleten XLIV 175, 1980, s. 459-466.
ÖZGÜÇ, Tahsin: "Kültepe Kazısında Bulunan Mermer İdol ve Hey-
kelcikler", Belleten, XXX. Sayı 81
ÖZGÜÇ, Tahsin: "Yortan Mezarlık Kültürüne Ait Yeni Buluntular",
Belleten VIII, 1944
Uygarlıklar Ülkesi Türkiye 1985.

HISTORIC PERIODS
Assyrian Trade Colony Period
Old Hittite and Hittite Empire Periods

AKURGAL, E: The Art of the Hittites, London, 1962,
ALP. Sedat Konya Civarında Karahöyük Kazılarında Bulunan Silindir
ve Damga Mühürler" T.T.K. Basımevi, Ankara, 1972
BERAN, T.: Die Hethitische Gluptik von Boğazköy I., Berlin, 1967
BITTEL, T.: Die Ruinen von Boğazköy, Berlin ve Leipzig, 1937.
BITTEL, K.: Boğazköy-Hattuşa III. Funde ous den Grabungen 1952
1955, Berlin, 1957
BITTEL, K.: Boğazköy-Hattuşa II. Die Hethitischen Grabfunde von
Osmankayası, Berlin, 1958
BITTEL, K. ve NAUMANN, A.: Boğazköy-Hattuşa, Stuttgart, 1952
BITTEL K. - R. NAUMANN - S.Otto, Yazılıkaya, Architectur, Kels-
bilder: Istanbuler Mitteilungen und Klemfundevdeg 61, Berlin-1941
BITTEL, Kurt. Die Hethiter Die Kunst Anateliens Von Ende Des
III. Bis Zum Anfang Des I. Jahrtausends vor Christus. München, C.H.
Beck, 1976
BLEGEN, C. W.: Troy III. The Sixth Settlements, Princeton, 1953
Troy IV. Settlements VII. and VIII, Princeton, 1958
EMRE, Kutlu: "The Pottery of The Assyrian Colonies Period Accord-
ing to The Building Levels of the Kanısh - Karum1" Anatolia
(Anadolu) VII, 1963 (1964), s. 87-99
EMRE, Kutlu : Anadolu Kurşun Figürinleri ve Taş Kalıpları, T.T.K.VI.
seri, 14, Ankara-1971
GARSTANG, J.: The Hittite Empire, London, 1929
GÜTERBOCK. T. M.: Guide to Ruins at Boğazkale, Berlin, 1966
GÜTERBOCK, H.G.: "Yazılıkaya", Mittelhungen der Deutschen
Orientgesellschaft 86, 1953.
GÜTERBOCK, H.G. ve: Halil Ethem Hatıra Kitabı, Ankara, 1947
GÜTERBOCK, H.G. ve ÖZGÜÇ, N· Ankara Bedesteninde Bulunan
Eti Büyük Salonunun Kılavuzu, İstanbul, 1946
KOŞAY, H.Z.: Türk Tarih Kurmu Tarafından Yapılan Alacahöyük
Harfiyatı, Ankara 1938
KOŞAY, H.Z.: Alacahöyük Kazısı 1936, Ankara, 1944
KOŞAY, Hamit Z.: Türk Tarih Kurumu Tarafından Yapılan Alaca-
höyük Kazısı 1937-1939'daki Çalışmalara ve Keşiflere Ait İlk La-
por, T.T.K.Y., seri V, no.5 Ankara-1951

KOŞAY, Hamit Z - AKOK Mahmut: **Türk Tarih Kurumu Tarafından Yapılan Alaca Höyük Kazısı** 1940-1948'deki Çalışmalara ve Keşiflere Ait İlk Rapor, T.T.K.Y, seri V, no. 6, Ankara-1966'

LAMB, W: **"Excavations at Kusura Near Afyonkarahisar"**, Archaeologia, 86, 1937

LLOYD, S. ve MELLAART J.: **Beycesultan II**, London, 1965

LLOYD, S. - **Early Highland People of Anatolia,** London - 1947

OSTEN, H.H. von der: **The Alishar Höyük Seasons 1930-32, Part I** The University Chicago Press, Illinois, 1937

OSTEN, Hans H. : **The Alishar Hüyük. Season of 1927, I.** The University of Chicago. Oriantal Institute Publications VI, Chica o-1930

ÖZGÜÇ, Tahsin: **Maşathöyük Kazıan ve Çevresindeki Araştırmalar** T.T.K.Y., Ankara-1973

ÖZGÜÇ, Tahsin : **Maşathöyük** II, T.T.K.Y., Ankara-1982

ÖZGÜÇ, Tahsin : **Kültepe-Kaniş II, Eski Yakındoğunun Ticaret Merkezinde Yeni Araştırmalar,** T.T.K.Y.V. dizi, sayı 41, Ankara 1986.

ÖZGÜÇ, Tahsin: **"VI. Trol'nin Anadolu Arkeolojisindeki Yeri"**, Belleten X, 1946.

ÖZGÜÇ, Tahsin: **1948 Kültepe Kazıları,** Ankara, 1950

ÖZGÜÇ, Tahsin: **Kültepe-Kaniş,** Ankara, 1959

ÖZGÜÇ, Tahsin ve ÖZGÜÇ, Nimet: **1949 Kültepe Kazısı,** Ankara 1953

ÖZGÜÇ, Tahsin: **"Bitik Vazosu",** Anatolia II (1957)

ÖZGÜÇ, Tahsin ve ÖZGÜÇ, Nimet: **1947 Karahöyük Kazısı,** Ankara, 1949

Late Hittite Period
Phrygian and Urartian Period

AKURGAL, Ekrem: **Phrygische Kunst,** A.Ü.D.T.C.F. yayınları, Ankara, 1955

AKURGAL, Ekrem: **Die Kunst Anatoliens,** Berlin 1961

AKURGAL, E.: **Spathethitische Bildkunst** Ankara, 1949

BALKAN, Kemal: **"Patnos'ta Keşfedilen Urartu Tapınağı ve Urartu Sarayı",** Atatürk Konferansları I, TTK. Basımevi, 1964

BERAN, T.: **Urartu, Kultur Geschichte des Alten Orient,** Stuttgart, 1961

BİLGİÇ, Emin-ÖĞÜN, Baki: **Adilcevaz Kef Kalesi Kazıları,** Anadolu 1965, Cilt 9, s.l.

BITTEL, K. ve OTTO, H.: **Demircihöyük. Eine vorgeschichtiche Ansieddlüng an der phrygisch-bithynischen Grenze,** Berlin, 1939

BOSSERT, ALKIM ve ÇABEL: **Karatepe Kazıları,** Türk Tarih Kurmu Basımevi, Ankara 1950

DELAPORTE, L.: **Malatya,** Paris, 1940

Elizabeth Simpson and Robert Payton, Royal Wooden : **Furniture from Gordion,** Archaelogy, volume 39. Number 6, s. 40, November, December 1986.

GELB, Ignace: **Hittite Hieroglyphic Monuments,** Chicago-1939

ÖĞÜN, Baki: **Urartu Halk Mezarları,** Cumhuriyetin 50. Yıldönümü Anma Kitabı, Ankara Üniversitesi DTCF Yayınları, 1974.

ÖZGÜÇ Tahsin: **"Anıtkabir Tümülüsleri",** Belleten, X. Sayı 41

ÖZGÜÇ, Tahsin: **Altıntepe Mimarlık Anıtları ve Duvar Resimleri,** Ankara 1966.

ÖZGÜÇ, Tahsin: **Altıntepe II Mezarlar, Depo Binası ve Fildişi Eserler,** Ankara, 1969.

PIOTROVSKY, Boris B., **The Ancient Civilization of Urartu,** Geneva 1969.

PIOTROVSKY, Boris B., **The Kingdom of Van and Its Art,** Urartu, New York 1967.

TEMİZER, Raci: **"Ankara'da Bulunan Kybele Kabartması",** Anatolia VII, s. 179-182, 1959

TEMİZER, Raci: **"Kayapınar Höyüğü",** Belleten XVIII, 1954

VAN LOON : **Maurits Nanning; Its Distinctive Traits in the Light of New Excavations,** İstanbul 1966.

WOOLLEY, C.L.: **Carchemisch Part II, London-1921.**

WOOLLEY, C.I.: Carchemisch Part III. The Excavations In The Inner Tawn, Inscriptions, London-1952.

YOUNG, R.S: **Three Great Early Tumuli,** University of Pennsylvania, 1981

YOUNG, R.S.: **"Gordion: Phrygian Construction and Architecture",** Expedition, The Bulletin of the University Museum of the University Pennsylvania.

YOUNG, R.S.: **Gordion Kazıları ve Müzesi Rehberi,** Ankara Turizmi Eski Eserleri Sevenler Derneği Yayınları

ANATOLIAN CIVILIZATIONS FROM THE 7th CENTURY B.C. ON

Akurgal, E.: **Die Kunst Anatoliens,** Berlin 1961; **Orient und Okzident** Baden-Baden 1966; **The Art of Greecese: The Orijins,** New York 1968; **Ancient Civilizations and Ruins of Turkey,** İstanbul 1985; **Griechische und Römische Kunst in der Turkei,** Hirmer 1987.

BEAN, G.E.: **Aegean Turkey,** London 1966

BOSCH.E.: **Quellen zur Geschichte der Stadt Ankara im Altertum,** T.T.K. Ankara 1967

COOK, J.: **Ionia and the East,** London 1962

DUYURAN, R.: **Batı Anadolu,** İstanbul 1948

ERZEN, A.: **İlk Çağda Ankara,** Ankara 1946

EYİCE, Semavi: **Ankara'nın Eski Bir Resmi,** Ank. 1972

FOSS, C., **Late Antigue and Byzantine,** Ankara, DOP 31, 1977

GALANTİ, Avram: **Ankara Tarihi** I-II, İst. 1946-1951

GÜLEKLİ, Nurettin Can: **Ankara Rehberi,** Ank. 1949

GÜLEKLİ, Nurettin Can: **Ankara Tarih ve Arkeoloji,** Ank. 1948

GÜLEKLİ, C.: **The guide of Ankara,** Ankara 1961

GÜRÜN, Ceyhan: Türk Hanlarının Gelişimi ve İstanbul Hanları Mimarisi, Ankara 1978

Hamit Zübeyr Koşay; **"Ankara Arkeoloji Müzesinin İlk Kuruluş Safhası İle İlgili Anılar",** Belleten C. XLIII. S. 170 Ankara 1979

İnan, J. - Rosenbaum, E., **Roman and Early Byzantine Portrait Soulpture** in Asie Minör. Oxford 1966

KOŞAY, H.Z.: **Augustus Tempel in Ankara,** Anatolia 2, 1957

KRENCKER-SCHEDE.: **Der Tempel in Ankara,** Berlin 1936

MAHMUT, A.: **Ankara Roma Hamamı,** Türk Ark Derg. 17, 1968

ÖNEY, Gönül: **Ankara'da Türk Devri Dini ve Sosyal Yapıları,** Ankara 1972.

ÖZDEMİR, Rıfat: **XIX. Yüzyılın İlk Yarısında Ankara,** Ank. 1986

THIS GUIDE BOOK HAS COMPILED FOR THE MUSEUM BY
THE DIRECTOR İ.TEMİZSOY,
ASSISTANT DIRECTORS M.KUTKAM, T.SAATÇİ,
MUSEUM ASSISTANTS
T.GÜNEL, A.TOKER, A.ÖZET, I.BİNGÖL, S.ÇELİKEL, H.KARADUMAN, B.KULAÇOĞLU,
N.KALAYCIOĞLU, D.MERMERCİ, A.KOPAR, M.ARSLAN, T.GÖKTÜRK, F.TAŞKIRAN,
S.EZER, K.ATA, G.ÜN, A.UZUNALİMOĞLU, E.YURTTAGÜL, Ç.TOPÇU, R.AKDOĞAN, S.MUTLU,
MUSEUM TECHNICIANS B.GÜNEL, M.KIRIŞCIOĞLU.

CHRONOLOGY OF ANATOLIA

PALEOLITHIC	
NEOLITHIC	8000 - 5500
CHALCOLITHIC	5500-3000
EARLY BRONZ AGE	3000-2000

PREHISTORIC PERIODS

ASSYRIAN TRADE COLONIES	1950-1750
OLD HITTITE	1750-1400
HITTITE EMPIRE	1400-1200
NEW HITTITE	1200- 700
PHRYGIAN "Early and Late Phase"	750-300
LYDIAN	700-300
URARTIAN	900-600
CARIAN/LYCIAN	700-300
IONIAN	1050-300
PERSIAN	545-333
HELLENISTIC	333- 30

HISTORIC PERIODS

ROMAN EMPIRE	30 B.C. -395
EARLY CHRISTIAN BYZANTIC PERIOD	330-1453
SELJUCK PERIOD	1071-1243
OTTOMAN PERIOD	1299-1920
REPUBLIC	1920-

Time scale (B.C. / A.D.): 8000 · 7000 · 6000 · 5000 · 4000 · 3000 · 2000 · 1000 · 0 · 1000 · 2000

FIND-PLACES OF OBJECTS IN THE MUSEUM		PALEOLITHIC	NEOLITHIC	CHALCOLITHIC	EARLY BRONZ AGE	ASSYRIAN TRADE COLONIES	HITTITE	NEW HITTITE	PHRYGIAN	URARTIAN
ACEMHÖYÜK	1						□			
ADİLCEVAZ	2									●
AHLATLIBEL	3				●					
ALACAHÖYÜK	4			▲	●	○	□		△	
ALİŞAR	5			▲		○			△	
ALTINTEPE	6									●
ANITKABİR	7				●				△	
ARSLANTEPE	8				●			◉		
BEYCESULTAN	9				●		□			
BOĞAZKÖY	10						□		△	
BOLU	11				●					
CANHASAN	12			▲						
ÇATALHÖYÜK	13		⬛							
ÇAVUŞTEPE	14									●
ELMALI	15				●					
EMİRDAĞ	16				●					
ESKİYAPAR	17		⬛		●		□			
ETİYOKUŞU	18				●					
FERZANT	19						□			
GORDİON	20								△	
HACILAR	21		⬛	▲						
HASANOĞLAN	22				●			◉		
HAVUZKÖY	23							◉		
HOROZTEPE	24				●					
ILICA	25						□			
İKİZTEPE	26									
İNANDIK	27						□			
KALINKAYA	28				●					
KARAİN	29	✿								
KARAOĞLAN	30				●					
KARAYAVŞAN	31				●					
KARAZ	32			▲						
KAYALIDERE	33									●
KARGAMIŞ	34							◉		
KÖYLÜTOLU	35						□			
KÜLTEPE	36				●	○	□			
MAHMATLAR	37				●					
MERZİFON	38				●					
PATNOS	39									●
PAZARLI	40								△	
SAKÇAGÖZÜ	41							◉		
SULTANHAN	42						□			
TİLKİTEPE	43									●
TOPRAKKALE	44									●
ÜNYE	45									●
VAN	46									●